The Ornamental Flower Garden And Shrubbery, Containing Coloured Figures And Descriptions Of The Most Beautiful And Curious Flowering Plants And Shrubs Cultivated In Great Britain: Selected From The Works Of John Lindley ... R. Sweet ... Professor D....

Anonymous

THE

ORNAMENTAL FLOWER GARDEN

AND SHRUBBERY,

CONTAINING

COLOURED FIGURES AND DESCRIPTIONS

OF THE MOST BEAUTIFUL AND CURIOUS

FLOWERING PLANTS AND SHRUBS

CULTIVATED IN GREAT BRITAIN,

SELECTED FROM THE WORKS OF

JOHN LINDLEY, Ph.D., F.R.S. & L.S.
R. SWEET, F.L.S., PROFESSOR D. DON,

ETC.

TO WHICH ARE ADDED ENGLISH DESCRIPTIONS,

AND THE MOST RECENT

Practical Hints on Culture, Propagation, etc.

BY

A PRACTICAL FLORICULTURIST.

TWO HUNDRED AND EIGHTY-EIGHT COLOURED PLATES,

DRAWN AND COLOURED AFTER NATURE.

COMPLETE IN FOUR VOLUMES.

VOL. IV.

LONDON:

G. WILLIS, GREAT PIAZZA, COVENT GARDEN.

1854.

INDEX.

⁂ THE NUMBERS REFER TO THE PLATES.

21

LILIUM THUNBERGIANUM.

Thunberg's Orange Lily.

Nat. Ord. LILIACEÆ.—LILYWORTS of Lindley.
Linnæan Class HEXANDRIA, Order MONOGYNIA.

LILIUM, Linnæus.—*Perianth* six-leaved, coloured, deciduous, the segments often ploughed at the base with a nectariferous furrow. *Stamens* six. *Style* elongate; *stigma* undivided. *Capsules* three-cornered, three-celled, three-valved, many seeded. *Seeds* smooth, with an obtuse margin, and a spongy testa.

L. Thunbergianum; stem villous above; leaves ovate-lanceolate, the inferior alternate, the superior whorled; flowers terminal erect; segments of the perianth sessile, spreading revolute at the apex glabrous within, many times longer than the stamens.

L. Thunbergianum, *Römer and Schultes Syst. Veg.* vi. 415. *Bot. Reg.* 1839, t. 38.

L. bulbiferum, *Thunberg in Act. Soc. Lin. Lond.* ii. 333.

L. philadelphicum, *Thunberg, Fl. Jap.*, 135.

A very handsome perennial with scaly bulbs, and an upright stem which is hairy in the upper part. The leaves on the lower part of the stem are alternate, while in the upper they are arranged in whorls; their form is ovate lance-shaped. The flowers are erect at the top of the stem, bright orange colour, the divisions of the perianth spreading smooth within, turned back at the point, and very much longer than the stamens.

This noble lily is one of those introduced to Europe from Japan by Dr. Siebold. The drawing was made in the nursery of Messrs. Rollissons, in June 1838. It was originally found by Thunberg, who first refered it to *L. philadelphicum*, although its sepals and petals are sessile; and subsequently to *L. bulbiferum*, although it has no bulbs, and is also destitute of the papillæ which render the inside of the flower of that species scabrous. It is doubtless a distinct species.

In cultivation this is a handsome frame or half-hardy bulb, growing about three feet high, and flowering from the beginning of July to the end of September, according to the manner in which it is treated. The bulbs should be fresh potted or planted in a pit well protected from wet, late in the autumn, or very early in the spring, in a mixture of sandy-peat, loam, and a small portion of well-rotted dung or leaf mould.

The soil in the pots or pit in which the fresh bulbs are planted, should be kept dry until they begin to grow, when water should be given, but rather sparingly at first, as there is more damage done to fresh imported or fresh potted bulbs by over watering, or keeping them damp during winter, or while they are in a dormant state, than by all other causes taken together.

The plant may be increased freely from every scale which the old bulb is composed of. These if separated, potted in sand, and placed in a gentle heat, will soon make plants, but they will not flower for two or three years.

The generic name comes from the Celtic *li*, signifying whiteness.

LILIUM _tenuifolium_

LILIUM TENUIFOLIUM.

Fine leaved-Lily.

———

Nat. Ord. LILIACEÆ.—LILYWORTS of Lindley.
Linnæan Class HEXANDRIA, Order MONOGYNIA.

———

LILIUM, Linnæus.—Perianth six-leaved, coloured, deciduous, the segments often ploughed at the base with a nectariferous furrow. *Stamens* six. *Style* elongate; *stigma* undivided. *Capsules* three-cornered, three-celled, three-valved, many seeded. *Seeds* smooth, with an obtuse margin, and a spongy testa.

———

L. tenuifolium; leaves narrow-linear; perianth revolute, the segments smooth with a two-valved furrow at the base; pistil twice shorter than the stamens; capsules roundish turbinate.

L. tenuifolium. *Fischer, MS., Schrad. Pl. Rar. Hort. Gœtt. Römer and Schultes Syst. Veg.* vii, 400. *D. Don in Sweet's Brit. Flow. Gard.* 2. s, t. 275.

L. linifolium, *Hornemann.*

———

The bulbs of this very handsome lily, are about the size of a walnut, rather coated than scaly. The stem is erect, from a span to a foot high, scarcely thicker than a crowquill, copiously besprinkled, as well as the rest of the plant, with minute crystalline dots, which give it a glaucous hue. The leaves are rather crowded, especially towards the top of the stem, disposed in a spiral manner, occasionally verticillate, very narrow-linear, bluntish, glaucous green, with a narrow silvery edge, marked above with a shallow furrow; the primordial ones lanceolate, acute, nerved, shining, attenuated

218

towards the base, and somewhat stalked. The flowers, mostly solitary in native specimens, often number from three to five, in cultivated plants, and are about half the size of those of *L. chalcedonicum*, and of the same rich minium red. The perianth is hexapetaloid, its divisions sessile, equal, oblong-lanceolate scarcely apiculate, revolute, glossy, furnished at the base with a rather wide furrow, the edges of which are thin, connivent, valvate, and papillose. The six stamens are equal; their filaments awlshaped, glabrous, pale red, connivent at the base, spreading at the top, shorter than the leaves of the perianth; their anthers incumbent, brown purple. The pistil is shorter than the stamens; the ovary triquetrous; the style triquetrous, about the length of the ovary; the stigma capitate, six-lobed, the lobes connivent and minutely papillose. The capsules are scarcely an inch long, rounded-oval or turbinate, membranous, three-celled, three-valved, the angles round, even, not keeled.

Our drawing of this fine species was taken from specimens which flowered in the Botanic Garden, Chelsea, where the plant was unusually luxuriant.

In delicacy of foliage, brilliancy of flowers, and gracefulness of habit, is not surpassed by any species of this highly ornamental genus. It is a native of the vast steppes of Siberia, where it appears to be abundant, but it is never found to extend beyond the 55th degree of north latitude. The bulbs are eaten by the wandering Tartars.

It had been confounded by Pallas, and most other botanists, with *L. pomponium*, from which it is easily distinguished by its smooth sepals, and by the more rounded angles of its capsule. Dr. Fischer first determined it to be a distinct species, and gave it the very apt name which it now bears. In *L. chalcedonicum* the sepals are warted, and the angles of the capsules keeled at the top. The whole plant is likewise much larger, the leaves broader, and the flowers nearly double the size.

It is a hardy bulb, requiring a light loamy soil, and to remain undisturbed in the soil. It is increased by offsets.

Lilium giganteum

U of M

LILIUM PEREGRINUM.

Narrow-sepalled White Lily.

———

Nat. Ord. LILIACEÆ—LILYWORTS of Lindley.
Linnæan Class HEXANDRIA, Order MONOGYNIA.

———

LILIUM, Linnæus.—*Perianth* six-leaved, coloured, deciduous, the segments often ploughed at the base with a nectariferous furrow. *Stamens* six. *Style* elongate; *stigma* undivided. *Capsules* three-cornered, three-celled, three-valved, many-seeded. *Seeds* smooth, with an obtuse margin, and a spongy testa.

———

L. peregrinum; leaves scattered linear-lorate; perianth bell-shaped drooping; segments, lanceolate, acute, glabrous, narrowed and distinct at the base; style triangular at the apex.

L. peregrinum, *Miller Dict.* n. 2. *Redouté Lil.* 199. *D. Don in Sweet's Brit. Fl. Gard.* 2, s., t. 367.

L. candidum. β. *Linn. Sp. Pl.* 433.

———

The stem of this species is straight, leafy, angular, glabrous, about three feet high, and about the thickness of one's finger. The leaves are alternate, linear-lorate, green, glabrous and shining, finely serrulate at the edges, furnished beneath with a prominent midrib, varying from three to six inches long, and about half an inch in breadth. The flower spike is terminal, composed of from eight to ten flowers. The perianth is drooping, campanulate, white, its segments three inches long, narrow, lanceolate, acute, erect, wavy and slightly twisted, attenuated and apart towards the base. The six stamens are considerably shorter than the perianth; their filaments awl-shaped, white; their anthers yellow, versatile, of two parallel, connate cells, opening lengthways. The ovary is obtusely six-angled; the style stout, cylindrical, white, pale green, and triangular at the apex, longer than the stamens; the stigma green, of three thick, fleshy, minutely papillose lobes.

This plant is an old inhabitant of the Dutch gardens, and, as appears from Miller, was long since introduced into our own, but, from the neglect into which the culture of hardy bulbous plants has fallen, it has almost wholly disappeared from collections. From the names applied to the plant by ancient authors, it would appear to have been originally obtained from Constantinople, which, coupled with the fact of its having preserved its characters unchanged for so long a period, is in favour of its claim to the rank of a species. It differs from *candidum* in its narrow sepals, attenuated and apart at the base, and by its style being furnished with three angles at the apex. The fig. 1 represents a sepal of *L. candidum*. The specimen represented in our plate, was derived from the collection of R. H. Jenkinson, Esq., at Norbiton Hall, near Kingston, in the month of July. The bulb had been imported from the Cape of Good Hope, the plant having been most probably introduced from Holland by some of the Dutch colonists.

It requires quite the same treatment as the common white lily; that is to say, the bulbs may be planted in the open borders, and in ordinarily favourable circumstances of soil and situation need no further attention. The less the bulbs are disturbed, the better, except for the purpose of propagation, which is effected by offsets.

LILIUM sanguineum.

LILIUM SANGUINEUM.

Blood-red Lily.

Nat. Ord. LILIACEÆ.—LILYWORTS of Lindley.
Linnæan Class HEXANDRIA, Order MONOGYNIA.

LILIUM, Linnæus.—*Perianth* six-leaved, coloured, deciduous, the segments often ploughed at the base with a nectariferous furrow. *Stamens* six. *Style* elongate; *stigma* undivided. *Capsules* three-cornered, three-celled, three-valved, many seeded. *Seeds* smooth, with an obtuse margin, and a spongy testa.

L. sanguineum; dwarf, smooth; leaves dense, somewhat whorled, ovate, lanceolate, acute; flowers erect, solitary, the segments of the perianth clawed, equalling the stamens, and having a downy nectariferous furrow.

L. sanguinem, *Lindley in Bot. Reg.* 1846, *t.* 50.

A dwarf showy half hardy bulb, with smooth stems, dense ovate-lanceolate leaves, and bearing an erect solitary but handsome blossom.

This species of Lily is remarkable for its dwarfness, not growing more then twelve or eighteen inches high, and for the vivid colour of its large solitary orange-red flower. It might be supposed to be a variety of *L. Thunbergianum*, but that plant has a tall hairy stem bearing several flowers of a larger size, with much shorter stamens, and a less brilliant colour. The divisions of the flower are, moreover, very distinctly stalked, which brings the species nearer to *L.*

220

philadelphicum, from which it is clearly distinguished by its upper leaves not being distinctly verticillate, and by its great woolly honey-furrow.

The species is said to be a plant of Japanese origin, and if so it is no doubt one of the discoveries of Dr. Siebold.

The drawing was made in the garden of the Horticultural Society of London, to which it had been presented by Mr. Groom of Walworth. It blooms in May or June.

It proves to be a half hardy bulb, growing freely in a light loamy or peat soil, to which has been added a small portion of well decomposed cow dung, or leaf mould. The bulbs, like those of the other kinds of Lily, always suffer when disturbed, and should therefore only be entirely removed from the soil when an increase is wanted. It is easily increased, either by parting the old bulbs or by the scales, each scale forming a plant, but then they require two or three years before they bloom.

LILIUM ROSEUM.

Rosy Indian Lily.

———

Nat. Ord. LILIACEÆ—LILYWORTS of Lindley.
Linnæan Class HEXANDRIA, Order MONOGYNIA.

———

LILIUM, Linnæus.—*Perianth* six-leaved, coloured, deciduous, the segments often ploughed at the base with a nectariferous furrow. *Stamens* six. *Style* elongate; *stigma* undivided. *Capsules* three-cornered, three-celled, three-valved, many seeded. *Seeds* smooth, with an obtuse margin and a spongy testa.

———

L. roseum; leaves alternate linear-acuminate; flowers racemose horizontal, bell-shaped; segments of the perianth obovate-lanceolate smooth within, recurved at the point, distinct to the base; stamens declinate, as long as the perianth; stigma three-lobed.

L. roseum, *Wallich Cat. No.* 5077.
L. Thomsonianum, *Lindley Bot. Reg.* 1845, t. 1.
Fritillaria Thomsoniana, *Royle Illust.* 388, t. 92.
Notholirion roseum, *Wallich, MS.*

———

A very handsome perennial, having a small oblong-ovate tunicated bulb. The stem is erect, smooth, a foot and a half high, bearing at its base in a crowded manner, the alternate sessile, linear-acuminate, grassy leaves, the lowermost of which are nearly or quite as long as the stem itself. The inflorescence is a terminal raceme of eight or ten, drooping, rosy-lilac flowers, of a form between funnel-shaped and bell-shaped, the segments of the perianth all distinct to the base, spathulate, with reflexed points, and furrowed (not nectariferous), white with a purple streak near the base. The six hypogynous stamens are as long as the perianth, and slightly declined, the anthers deep-purple, the pollen orange-red. The ovary is oblong-obtuse, the style as long as the stamens, and declined with them, the stigma three-lobed.

This beautiful plant is a native of the northern provinces of British India—Gossain Than, Kamaon, Mussooree, and Almora. Our figure was made from a plant cultivated by Messrs. Loddiges, with whom it opened its sweet-scented flowers in a green-house in April, 1844.

Its affinities have been variously stated by those botanists who have described it. On this point Dr. Lindley remarks: "It was first seen by the people employed by Dr. Wallich who regarded it as a Lily. Prof. Royle afterwards referred it to Fritillaria; but its floral leaves have not the honey-pore which is essential to that genus. In fact it is far too near in structure to the common white Lily, to allow of its being distinguished generically. Its delicate rose-coloured flowers offer however a very marked feature of distinction. The specimen from which the figure was taken had been grown in a pot, and was by no means in good health. It would doubtless become much larger if treated with the care that is bestowed on the Japan Lilies. Fig. 1. represents the base of one of the floral leaves, to show that there is no trace of a honey-pore."

It is a very handsome half-hardy bulb, requiring a light rich loamy soil, and the protection of a cool frame in the winter and spring months. It flowers in May, and is increased by dividing the bulbs or by seeds. The seeds should be sown when ripe, in pans filled with light sandy loam and leaf-mould, and placed in a cold pit or frame, and kept rather dry at first; afterwards they should be rather freely supplied during the growing season. The young plants should not be removed from the seed pan before the second season, and then in a growing state. Seedling plants grow slowly, and take some years before they bloom.

LILIUM. *speciosa.*

LILIUM SPECTABILE.

Showy Siberian Lily.

———

Nat. Ord. LILIACEÆ.—LILYWORTS of Lindley.
Linnæan Class HEXANDRIA, Order MONOGYNIA.

———

LILIUM, Linnæus.—Perianth six-leaved, coloured, deciduous, the segments often ploughed at the base with a nectariferous furrow. *Stamens* six. *Style* elongate ; *stigma* undivided. *Capsules* three-cornered, three-celled, three-valved, many seeded. *Seeds* smooth, with an obtuse margin, and a spongy testa.

———

L. spectabile ; leaves subternate or scattered linear, faintly three-nerved, the upper ones slightly tomentose at the margins ; peduncles tomentose ; perianth erect, scabrous within.

L. spectabile, *Fisher. Link. Enum.* i. 321. *Sweet's Brit. Fl. Gard.* t. 75.
L. pensylvanicum, *Ker Bot. Mag.* t. 872.
L. dauricum, *Ker Bot. Mag.* t. 1210, note.

———

A showy hardy bulb. The stem is erect, from one to two feet high. The leaves ternate, or scattered, linear-lanceolate, acute, faintly three-nerved, the lower ones smooth and glossy, the upper ones slightly tomentose, particularly at the margins. The flowers terminal, from one to six in number, umbellate, of an orange colour, on peduncles unequal in length, densely tomentose, and often one-leaved. The perianth is hexapetaloid, its segments between ovate and lanceolate, gradually attenuated to the base and point, in which respect it differs from *L. bulbiferum, L. croceum,* &c. ; the inside is rough warted, and spotted with black or dark purple. Stamens six, their

222

filaments smooth purple, attached to the base of the perianth, and joined to the back of the anther. The style is purple, three-channelled, thickened upwards; stigma clubbed, tri-sulcate.

Our drawing was taken in the month of July from a plant at the garden of the Apothecaries' Company at Chelsea, where it was growing vigorously in the open border. It is a native of Davuria.

It is quite hardy, and thrives well in the common garden soil, flowering the latter end of June, or the beginning of July. It increases pretty freely by offsets from the bulbs; and it also ripens seeds, which should be sown as soon as gathered, as they then vegetate immediately.

The various hardy Lilies are among the most showy of the bulbous plants known in our gardens, and are one and all deserving of being collected and cultivated. There are few or none but may be grown in well-drained soil, if the surface is well sheltered by litter in the winter season. The majority, especially the hardier ones, no doubt succeed best in rich porous loam, whilst for the tenderer species peat soil, or at least a portion of peat soil, is doubtless preferable, though perhaps more on account of its mechanical influence than from any other cause.

YUCCA GLAUCESCENS.

Glaucescent Adam's Needle.

Nat. Ord. LILIACEÆ.—LILYWORTS of Lindley.
Linnæan Class HEXANDRIA, Order MONOGYNIA.

YUCCA, Linnæus.—Perianth campanulate, six-parted, regular, the segments erect, not nectariferous. *Stamens* six, the filaments thickened above; anthers small. *Stigmas* sessile. *Capsule* oblong, obtusely three-cornered, three-celled, three-valved, many seeded. *Seeds* flat.

Y. *glaucescens;* leaves linear-lanceolate entire concave glaucescent straight, the margin sparingly filamentose; inner segments of the perianth half as broad again as the outer.

Y. glaucescens, *Haworth. Supp. Pl. Suc.* 35.

A stemless species. The leaves spread around the stem, the middle ones being upright, from twelve to eighteen inches long, and one broad linear-lanceolate, straight, rigid, tapering at both ends, concave, particularly towards the point, which terminates in a sharp horny spine; they are of a dull glaucous colour, the margin entire, with here and there a slender white somewhat twisted thread. The flower-stem rises from three to four feet in height, and is much branched towards the top, the branches short, angular, channelled, densely covered with a short white down, and thickly clothed with flowers. The latter are generally in pairs, the terminal ones

223

solitary, greenish white tinged with yellow. Bracts sphace-late, membranaceous, sheathing at the base, ovate-lanceolate, concave, acute, of a grey brown, streaked with numerous darker lines. The peduncles are short cylindrical, a little bent when in flower, downy. The perianth is campanulately spreading, divided into six segments nearly to the base; the segments thick and succulent, the three inner ones half as broad again as the outer ones. Stamens six, inserted in the base of the perianth; their filaments gradually thickening upwards, a little longer than the ovary; the anthers small in proportion, sagittate, attached at the base, blunt-pointed. The ovary is superior, bluntly three-sided; style none; stigmas three, sessile, channelled inwards, with retuse points.

This plant is a native of North America, and was introduced by the late Mr. Lyons, from whom the late Mr. Colvill purchased the plants from which our drawing was taken. It is a fine stately perennial plant when in flower; in rich soil attaining the height of three or four feet. The plants continue in bloom from the beginning of August till the middle of October. The present species is quite hardy, and will succeed well in any common garden soil. It may be increased abundantly by the suckers from the roots.

The Yuccas all prefer a dryish and deep sandy loam in which they thrive admirably. They are all highly ornamental from the exotic aspect they bear, and should be freely introduced in mixed flower borders, on rockeries, on lawns, and in similar situations where there is space for their development.

224

YUCCA *acuminata*

H. Smith Del.   Wedwood Sc

YUCCA ACUMINATA.

Tapering-flowered Adam's Needle.

Nat. Ord. LILIACEÆ.—LILYWORTS of Lindley.
Linnæan Class HEXANDRIA, Order MONOGYNIA.

YUCCA, Linnæus.—Perianth campanulate, six-parted, regular, the segments erect, not nectariferous. *Stamens* six, the filaments thickened above; anthers small. *Stigmas* sessile. *Capsule* oblong, obtusely three-cornered, three-celled, three-valved, many seeded. *Seeds* flat.

Y. *acuminata;* stem erect shrubby; leaves lanceolate entire marginate, smooth rigid; concave above; flowers panicled; bracts linear-lanceolate acuminate, longer than the pedicels: segments of the perianth lanceolate-elliptic acuminate.

Y. acuminata, *Sweet in Brit. Fl. Garden,* t. 195.

In this species of Yucca, the stem is short and thick, frutescent, scarcely a foot in height. The leaves are numerous rigid straight lanceolate concave, quite entire and smooth at the edges, and terminating in a long brown sharp spine, more or less attenuated towards the base, tapering at the point, palish green with a brown margin; the lower ones spreading, the upper ones erect and imbricate. The flower-stem is between three and four feet high, angular, and striate, alternately branched, its branches acutely angular, spreading. The flowers are solitary, alternate, nodding, not in pairs.

224

Bracts two, narrow lanceolate, taper-pointed, brown deciduous, one of them longer than the nodding pedicels, the other scarcely its length. The perianth is deeply six-parted; the segments lanceolate, or narrowly elliptic, tapering to a long slender incurved point, striated with numerous faint lines, greenish white tinged with brownish purple; the inner ones broadest. Stamens six, inserted in the base of the perianth; the filaments roughly pubescent thickening upwards the points bent outwards; the anthers smallish, ovate. The ovary is superior, three-sided; the stigmas three, with two-lobed points.

Our drawing of this handsome species of Yucca, was made in the month of October, at Lavender-hill, Wandsworth. According to Sweet, it had been supposed to be a weak plant of *Y. gloriosa*, but appeared to him a distinct species as was satisfactorily ascertained by a comparison with that species. The perianth in *Y. gloriosa* has broad ovate segments, as represented in the *Botanical Magazine*, while those of the present species are narrow and acuminate. The leaves in *Y. acuminata* are also much less, as is the whole plant, the trunk being scarcely a foot in height. Sweet considers it more nearly related to *Y. rufocincta* than to any other, but from that, it is distinguished at first sight by the leaves being straight and rigid; those of *Y. rufocincta* being weak and flaccid, drooping from about the middle, and of a different form.

The whole of the species thrive well in a rich light soil, and are increased by the suckers at the roots.

Yucca is the name borne by some of these plants in Peru.

225

E.D.Smith Del.   YUCCA. *puberula.*   Weddall Sc.

YUCCA PUBERULA.

Downy Adam's Needle.

———

Nat. Ord. LILIACEÆ.—LILYWORTS of Lindley.
Linnæan Class HEXANDRIA, Order MONOGYNIA.

———

YUCCA, Linnæus.—*Perianth* campanulate six-parted regular, the segments erect, not nectariferous. *Stamens* six, the filaments thickened above; *anthers* small. *Stigmas* sessile. *Capsule* oblong, obtusely three-cornered, three-celled, three-valved, many-seeded. *Seeds* flat.

———

Y. puberula; stemless; leaves spreading, lanceolate or linear-lanceolate, plane, glaucous, concave at the apex, mucronulate, the margin filamentose; flower stem erect, paniculately branched, the branches flexuose and downy; segments of the perianth elliptic-lanceolate acute.

Y. puberula, *Haworth Phil. Mag.* 1828, p. 186. *Sweet in Brit. Fl. Gard. t.* 257.

———

This species is a stemless perennial, producing numerous suckers. The leaves are from a foot to eighteen inches in length, an inch and half in breadth, spreading, smooth, glaucous, flat or a little concave at the points; they are of a thin weak texture, generally erect, or spreading straight, the points of some of the old ones slightly bent downwards; in form lanceolate or linear-lanceolate, tapering to the base and point, and terminated by a softish brown spine; their margins are smooth, edged with a yellowish brown membrane, which tears up irregularly in the form of threads. The flower-stem is erect or slightly flexuose, leafy below the branches, from four to four and a half feet in height, clothed with a woolly pubescence which increases in thickness on the upper part of the stem; the branches are much bent or flexuose and densely clothed with a soft woolly down. The flowers are crowded, lemon-scented, white tinged with green; they are produced in threes at the base of the branches, in pairs higher up, and towards the point solitary. The bracts are broadly lanceolate; the peduncles nodding, less pubescent than the branches. The perianth is six-parted nearly to the base, inflated in the middle, slightly pubescent outside, the segments elliptic-lanceolate, acute, the three inner ones broadest, the points generally curved inwards. Stamens six, inserted in the base of the perianth; filaments densely clothed with long pellucid fleshy hairs, scarcely as long as the ovary, thickening at the points when the anthers burst; anthers sagittate. Ovary six-furrowed, smooth; stigma three-sided, deeply three-furrowed, three-parted about half way down, the points two-lobed or emarginate.

The drawing of the plant was made from specimens communicated from the Bristol Nursery, where it was believed to have been received from North America. Haworth considered it a new species. It is most nearly related to *Y. flaccida* and *Y. glaucescens*, particularly to the former, which has also pubescent flower-stems, but differs from the present by its flaccid leaves all bending downwards from about the middle, from which circumstance it has been confounded with *Y. recurvifolia* in many collections; that however is a different plant, of strong growth, with green leaves, and not filamentose at the margins, or very rarely so.

The present species thrives well in the open borders in the common garden soil, and makes a fine appearance when in bloom. It is increased by the suckers from the root. They all prefer deep sandy loam and are highly ornamental objects for the mixed flower borders, for rockeries, lawns, or similar situations where there is space for their development.

2.261

226

AMARYLLIS Barkeriana.

AMARYLLIS BANKSIANA.

Banks's Amaryllis.

———◆———

Nat. Ord. AMARYLLIDACEÆ.—AMARYLLIDS of Lindley.
Linnæan Class HEXANDRIA, Order MONOGYNIA.

———

AMARYLLIS, Linnæus.—*Perianth* hexapetaloid, the tube narrow funnel-shaped, the segments of the limb reflex. *Stamens* six, opposite the segments of the perianth, the pelatine inserted at the base of the segments, the sepaline inserted lower; *anthers* incumbent. *Ovary* triangularly obovate. *Capsules* obovate three-celled, three-valved, disposed to burst prematurely. *Seeds* subglobose.

———

A. Banksiana; leaves erect obtuse glaucescent, shorter than the many-flowered scape; umbel divaricate; peduncles slender, three times as long as the flowers; perianth deep rose.
A. Banksiana, *Lindley in Bot. Reg.* 1842, t. 11.
A. grandiflora, *var.* Banksiana, *Herbert Amaryllidaceæ*, 279, t. 32.

———

A very handsome bulbous plant, with broadish blunt erect-growing leaves issuing from the crown of the bulb, which also produces by their side a stout scape terminating in an umbel of numerous deep rose coloured handsome blossoms.
This beautiful plant was imported from the Cape, by J. H. Slater, Esq. of Newick Park, near Uckfield, from whose plant our drawing was made. It appears to have been introduced to this country many years ago, a leaf and flower of it in the Banksian herbarium having been obtained from Kew Gardens. It is closely allied to *A. grandiflora*, *(Bot.*
226

Reg. t. 1335) but the shorter peduncles and different colour and expansion of the flowers, serve to distinguish it. In our figure however, the inflorescence is too compact. Fig. 1. represents a vertical section of one cell of the ovary, and fig. 2. a transverse section of the whole ovary, showing, what is not uncommon in the Amaryllidaceous order, that the dissepiments merely touch each other in the axis, without being actually united.

It is a greenhouse plant, and grows well in a rich free loamy soil. The principal points to be attended to in its cultivation are to keep it in a vigorous healthy state while growing by placing it in a light situation, and giving it plenty of water, and when the leaves die off to keep it warm and dry. It flowers in the autumn, and is multiplied by offsets, or by seeds, when they can be ripened.

According to Dr. Herbert (*Amaryllidaceæ*, p. 278), the very large bulbs sometimes imported of species closely allied to this—*A. Josephiniana* and *Brunsvigia multiflora*—may be one hundred years old. "As they sprout but once a year," he writes, " nothing can be done to accelerate their growth, beyond keeping them in a healthy and vigorous state: for which purpose the bulb must be kept *under ground*, with the neck perhaps above ground; but of that I entertain great doubts. If the whole bulb is exposed, it imbibes moisture from the atmosphere in the season of rest, which becomes fatal to it, and I have found the seedlings of which the neck has never been raised above ground in the safest state. A rich light loam and abundance of water in winter, perfect rest and dry heat in summer, are necessary. I lost my bulb of *A. grandiflora* very soon, and I fear all that were imported at the same time have been also lost, in consequence of the dangerous practice of keeping the bulb above ground."

HYLUCTAMA *melaanoma*

HYDROTÆNIA MELEAGRIS.

Checquered Waterband.

———

Nat. Ord. IRIDACEÆ—IRIDS of Lindley.
Linnæan Class MONADELPHIA, Order TRIANDRIA.

———

HYDROTÆNIA, Lindley.—Perianth bell-shaped subequal, the petals clawed and banded above the claw with a triangular zone, which is honey-bearing at the apex. *Stamens* three, monadelphous, opposite the sepals ; *anthers* sessile, affixed by their base, the cells margined by the connectives. *Ovary* with a free conical apex ; *ovules* numerous inserted in the central angle of the cells ; *style* filiform trifid at the apex, the segments three-parted linear convolute, the lateral alternating with, the intermediate opposite to and shorter than the anthers.

———

H. meleagris.
   H. meleagris, *Lindley Bot. Reg.* 1838, *misc.* 1828 ; 1842, t. 39.

———

A curious bulbous plant growing a foot and a half high, the stems bearing one sword-shaped leaf, and terminating in a foliaceous hooded spathe containing four or five very fugacious flowers borne on slender pendulous stalks. The perianth is bell-shaped brownish-purple externally, paler and spotted within; the petals have at their base a triangular glandular bar, the point of which is directed upwards and secretes honey, and when fresh is slightly excavated into hollows "resembling a row of pearls placed on a pale yellow ground." The name of the genus refers to this circumstance of a band secreting fluid.

227

The plant was gathered on mountain pastures near the Real Del Monte mines in Mexico, and was imported by J. Rogers, Esq. Jun. of Sevenoaks. The accompanying figure was taken from a plant which flowered in the garden of the Horticultural Society.

Although closely allied to the genus *Sisyrinchium* it has quite a different habit, imitating as it were the *Fritillaria* in the Amaryllidaceous order; it differs further in having the anthers opposite the primary lobes of the style. Its appearance is by no means attractive, but the interior of the flower, when carefully examined, will be found to exhibit beauties of no common kind. The curious watery band, which glitters as if covered with dew, or as if constructed out of broken rock crystal, is a most exquisite object. The stigmas too are extremely remarkable; each divides into two arms, which are rolled up as if forming a gutter, with a dense mass of bright papillæ at the end, and a single tooth on the inner edge; between the arms stands a short mucro which is free from glands, and forms a minute horn; it is by the union of three such stigmata that the nine lobes of the style are produced. Fig. 1. represents a petal seen from within; 2. is a view of the column, and 3. of the style and stigmata apart.

Hydrotænia is a greenhouse bulb of which the cultivation is extremely simple. The pots in which it is kept ought to receive no water after the leaves have withered in autumn, until they begin to grow again in spring. A dry shelf in the greenhouse is an excellent place to keep it during the winter. When it commences its growth it ought then to be placed in a light situation, and to be watered gently at first and then freely afterwards, when it will soon form its leaves and flowers. It succeeds perfectly in equal parts of loam, leaf-mould and sand, and is multiplied by offsets or seeds.

The genus is named from *hydor* water, and *tainia* a band, in allusion to the bar of shining water-like tissue which is placed on the petals in the form of two sides of a triangle.

228

228

GLADIOLUS. *alatus.*

E.D.Smith Del.

Weddel sc.

GLADIOLUS ALATUS.

Winged-flowered Cornflag.

Nat. Ord. IRIDACEÆ.—IRIDS of Lindley.
Linnæan Class TRIANDRIA, Order MONOGYNIA.

GLADIOLUS, Tournefort.—Perianth corolline superior irregular; *tube* rather terete; *limb* six-parted, two-lipped, the lobes unequal. *Stamens* three inserted in the tube of the perianth, erect or subsecund, included or exserted; *filaments* filiform; *anthers* linear, affixed by the back above the base. *Ovary* inferior obtusely three-sided, three-celled; *ovules* numerous in many rows in the central angles of the cells, pendulous, anatropous; *style* filiform; *stigmas* three petaloid-dilated. *Capsule* membranous three-celled, loculicidally three-valved. *Seeds* numerous pendulous, flat, compressed, or more rarely globose.

G. alatus; leaves rigid nerved-plicate downy; upper segments of the perianth obovate erect-recurved, the lateral rhombeo-ovate spreading, recurved at the point, the lower spathulate acute dependent.

G. alatus, *Linnæus, Sp. Pl.* 53. *Bot. Mag.* 586. *Sweet's Brit. Fl. Gard.* t. 187.

Hebea alata, *Persoon.*

A very handsome perennial plant having small flattish corms or bulb-tubers, clothed with a deciduous brown fibrous coat, and rigid narrowly ensiform, or lanceolate leaves, the outer ones blunt the inner more acute, strongly nerved and plaited, tapering to the base and sheathing the stem, pale green, the nerves pubescent. The scape is longer than the leaves, flexuose, sharply triquetrous, the leaves and sheaths

228

decurrent from one joint to the next. The spathe is two-valved, the outer one half as long again as the inner, which is convolute and of a thinner texture. The perianth is irregular, widely spreading, the tube very short, about five times shorter than the spathe; the upper segment of the limb erect, or slightly recurved, obovate tapering to the base, bright orangy scarlet lighter in the centre and much veined; those at the sides rhomboid broad ovate, spreading with the points recurved, and having a dark purple line down the centre, the three lower ones connected at the base, spatulate, acute, golden yellow except at the points, which are scarlet. Stamens three, inserted in the throat of the tube; filaments bent round like an arch, villosely hairy; anthers linear, sagittate at the base, with cream-coloured pollen. Style very hairy, bent downward in the same direction as the stamens; stigmas three, spreading, the points spatulate and fimbriate.

This handsome species which had been lost to our collections, for many years, was reintroduced from the interior of the Cape by Mr. Synnot. Our drawing was made from plants which flowered at the nursery of Mr. Colville.

The present plant requires precisely the same sort of treatment as *G. viperatus*, (t. 229) to which it is nearly related. An equal mixture of turfy loam, peat and sand, will suit them; and if allowed to remain in the open ground all the winter, they will require to be covered in frosty weather. It increases very freely by the offsets from its bulbs, which are produced in abundance.

GLADIOLUS. *vittatus.*

GLADIOLUS VIPERATUS.

Perfumed Corn-flag.

Nat. Ord. IRIDACEÆ.—IRIDS of Lindley.
Linnæan Class TRIANDRIA, Order MONOGYNIA.

GLADIOLUS, Tournefort.—Perianth corolline superior irregular; *tube* rather terete; *limb* six-parted, two-lipped, the lobes unequal. *Stamens* three inserted in the tube of the perianth, erect or subsecund, included or exserted; *filaments* filiform; *anthers* linear, affixed by the back above the base. *Ovary* inferior obtusely three-sided, three-celled; *ovules* numerous in many rows in the central angles of the cells pendulous, anatropous; *style* filiform; *stigmas* three petaloid dilated. *Capsule* membranous three-celled, loculicidally three-valved. *Seeds* numerous pendulous, flat-compressed, or more rarely globose.

G. *viperatus ;* leaves ensiform glaucescent striate-nerved, acute; scape simple flexuose subcernuous; upper segments of the perianth arched-incurved, the three outer rhombeo-ovate spreading acute, the two inner spathulate acute dependent.

G. viperatus, *Ker in Bot. Mag.* t. 688. *Sweet in Brit. Fl. Gard.* t. 156.
G. alatus, *Willdenow; Jacquin ; not of others.*

A bulb-tuberous perennial, with distichous rather glaucous ensiform, acute, strongly nerved leaves, scarcely as long as the scape, which is simple, more or less flexuose, bending forward, and bearing eight to ten flowers in a compact secund spike. The spathe is two-valved, inclosing the tube of the flower, the outer lanceolate, acute, the inner much shorter bifid. The perianth is tubular, six-cleft, the tube short, widening upwards; the upper segment of the limb arched, and incurved, spathulate, narrow at the base, the point scarcely acute; the two middle, and the lower outer segments are rhomboid-ovate, acute, the margins a little crumpled, greenish ash colour with a purple line down the centre of each, and a large brownish yellow mark near the base of the lower one; the two inner lower ones are spathulate, acute, narrowing to the base, ash-coloured, like the other segments, but marked with a purple mark broad at the base, and terminated in a sharp point. Stamens three, inserted in the tube, and bent down like the upper segment; the filaments smooth, attached to the anthers a little above their base; the anthers linear, sagittate at the base, two-celled, with yellow pollen. Style smooth, curved like the stamens, and about their length; stigmas three, the points bilamellate and fringed.

This curious and delightfully fragrant plant had been lost from our collections, until reintroduced from the Cape by Mr. Synnot. It may be grown as freely as the common *Tigridia pavonia*, either in the open air, or in a pit covered with lights in winter; either of which modes of treatment will cause the bulbs to grow stronger, and produce large flowers than if grown in pots. If they are required to be grown in pots, they should be planted in composts of one third fine sand, rather more than a third of light turfy loam, and the rest peat, all mixed well together, the pots to be well drained with a handful of potsherds, broken small, that the wet may pass off readily. As soon as they have done flowering, and the stalks begin to decay, they should have no more water given them, but the pots may be laid on their sides, or be placed in a frame under lights, not too much exposed to the sun; and care must be taken that the mice do not get at them, as they are apt to make great havoc amongst roots of this kind. In October they should be re-potted and placed in a frame where frost will not get at them. Those planted in beds in the open air or in frames, will require exactly the same treatment as *Ixias* and other Cape bulbs.

230

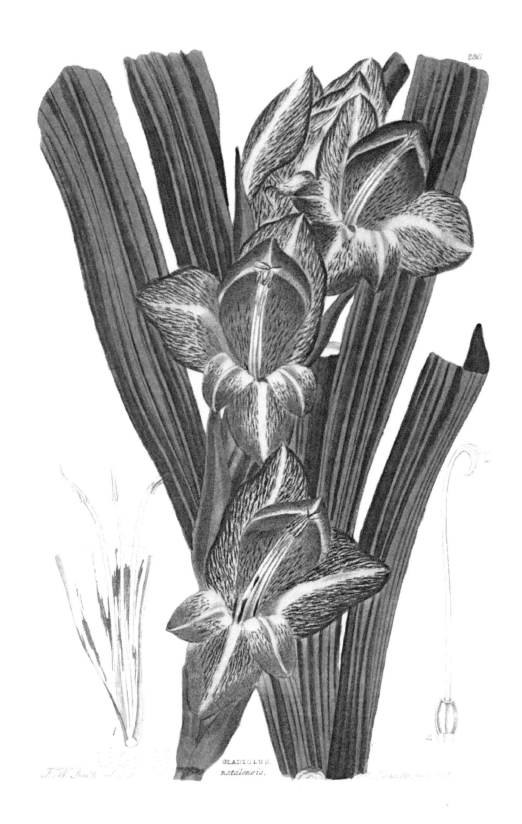

GLADIOLUS.
natalensis.

GLADIOLUS NATALENSIS.

Natal Corn-flag.

Nat. Ord. IRIDACEÆ.—IRIDS of Lindley.
Linnæan Class TRIANDRIA, Order MONOGYNIA.

GLADIOLUS, Tournefort.—Perianth corolline superior irregular; *tube* rather terete; *limb* six-parted two-lipped, the lobes unequal. *Stamens* three inserted in the tube of the perianth, erect or subsecund, included or exserted; *filaments* filiform; *anthers* linear, affixed by the back above the base. *Ovary* inferior obtusely three-sided, three-celled; *ovules* numerous in many rows in the central angles of the cells, pendulous, anatropous; *style* filiform; *stigmas* three petaloid-dilated. *Capsule* membranous three-celled, loculicidally three-valved. *Seeds* numerous pendulous, flat, compressed, or more rarely globose.

G. natalensis; segments of the perianth elliptic abruptly mucronate, the three upper large and conniving into a helmet; throat of the tube ventricose six-furrowed; spathe longer than the tube, the inner one bicuspidate.

G. natalensis, *Reinwardt MS. D. Don in Sweet's Brit. Fl. Gard.* 2. s, t. 281.

G. psittacinus, *Hooker Bot. Mag.* t. 3032. *Bot. Reg.* t. 1442.

A beautiful upright growing perennial, furnished with corms or bulb-tubers. The stems are straight cylindrical glaucous green, three feet or more in height, with broadish ensiform acuminate, erect, grass green leaves, two or three feet long, and having four or five prominent pale ribs, and a white cartilaginous border. The flowers are the largest of

230

the genus, deep orange scarlet, mottled with yellow, about four inches long, disposed in a terminal one-sided spike. The two spathes are convolute broadly lanceolate pointed, pale green, striated, considerably longer than the tube, the inner one shorter, and cloven at the top. The tube of the perianth is pale green, angular, stained with purple, ventricose and furrowed above, with six broad elevated rounded ridges; its throat about the length of the tube. The three upper segments are broadly elliptical, abruptly bristle-pointed, connivent in the form of a helmet; the lower one is of the same shape and colour, but smaller; the inner pair four or five times smaller, paler, with a longer point. The three filaments are trique-trous, glabrous pale yellow, bearing linear-oblong, incumbent, yellow emarginate anthers, sagittate at the base. The ovary is turbinate, nearly round, with six shallow furrows; the style filiform, glabrous, furrowed; the stigma of three laterally compressed, recurved, blunt, papillose segments. The tube of the perianth secretes abundantly a honey-like fluid.

A native of the banks of Natal River, which falls into the Indian Ocean in about 29° 30′ south latitude, and which constitutes the northern boundary of Natal, on the south east coast of Caffraria. The country was so called by the Portuguese navigators, who discovered it on Christmas day in the year 1498.

We owe the introduction of this truly magnificent species to Professor Reinwardt of Leyden, who liberally distributed bulbs of it to various collections both in this country and on the continent. It is by far the largest in growth, and in the beauty of its flowers it is not surpassed by any others of the genus. Our drawing was taken from a plant which flowered in the open border at the Exotic Nursery, King's Road, Chelsea, in the beginning of August.

The plant seems to be quite as hardy as the *G. byzantinus*, and requires the same soil and treatment as that species; that is to say, it thrives in the open borders in situations where the soil is warm and dry from efficient drainage, and in such situations requires to be seldom disturbed. If the soil is not well drained there is risk of the corms perishing in winter, and in this case, they should be taken up in autumn when the leaves are quite ripe, stored in dry sand, and replanted in February or early in March. The best soil is a rich sandy loam. They increase both by seeds and offsets.

231.

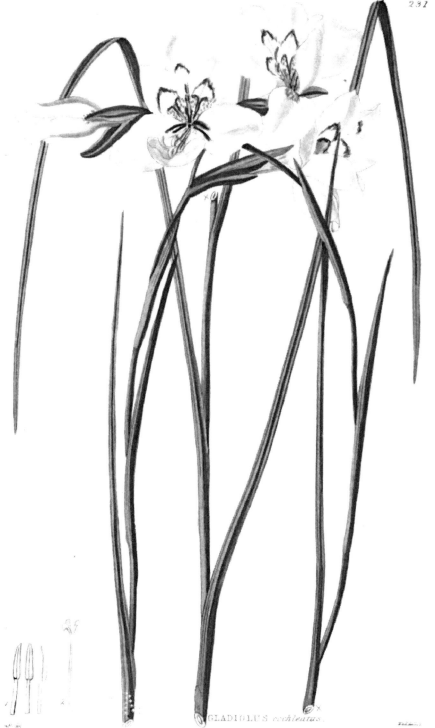

GLADIOLUS cochleatus.

GLADIOLUS COCHLEATUS.

Spoon-lipped Corn-flag.

———

Nat. Ord. IRIDACEÆ.—IRIDS of Lindley.
Linnæan Class TRIANDRIA, Order MONOGYNIA.

———

GLADIOLUS, Tournefort.—Perianth corolline superior irregular; *tube* rather terete; *limb* six-parted, two-lipped, the lobes unequal. *Stamens* three inserted in the tube of the perianth, erect or subsecund, included or exserted; *filaments* filiform; *anthers* linear, affixed by the back above the base. *Ovary* inferior obtusely three-sided, three-celled; *ovules* numerous in many rows in the central angles of the cells, pendulous, anatropous; *style* filiform; *stigmas* three petaloid-dilated. *Capsule* membranous three-celled, loculicidally three-valved. *Seeds* numerous pendulous, flat, compressed, or more rarely globose.

———

G. cochleatus; leaves narrow-linear elongate, two-nerved rigid glaucescent; scape simple slender; segments of the perianth elliptic ovate obtuse, the upper smaller painted with red within, the lowest adscendent spoon-like concave; tube short, much shorter than the spathe.
G. cochleatus, *Sweet in Brit. Fl. Gard.* 2. s., t. 140.

———

In this species the stem is slender, a foot and a half high somewhat glaucous, and leafy all the way up, the leaves varying in length upwards, and being somewhat glaucous; all narrow-linear elongated straight rigid and tapering to a slender point, the lower ones two-nerved with the nerves and margins thickened and prominent, sheathing the stem a considerable distance up. The flowers are few on a simple scape; the spathe is two-valved, the outer one being much longer
231

than the inner, both longer than the tube of the perianth, glaucous, and striated. The perianth is snowy white, with a very short tube; the three upper segments of the limb about half the size of the lower ones, and more erect, but slightly bent backwards; the outer of the three, is wedge-shaped, with a red mark in the shape of an opened pair of compasses and which nearly joins two crimson lines which proceed to the base, and there become connected; the two inner are elliptically ovate, also marked with an open compass-shaped red mark, and below this are two red marks, running down the centre of the segment, and extending nearly the width of the upper mark; the two outer lower segments are very large and spreading, elliptical-ovate, the points somewhat reflexed, marked with two red lines, from a little below the middle to the bottom, the upper line shortest; the lower segment is obovately ovate, spoon-shaped, hollow, broad at the point, becoming a little undulate. Stamens three, slightly ascending, shorter than the style; anthers linear, with straw-coloured pollen. Stigma three-cleft, the segments very slender at the base, but dilated at the ends.

The hollow spoon-shaped ascending lower segment of the perianth, appears to distinguish the present from every other species; Sweet suggests, that it is most nearly related to *G. debilis (Bot. Mag.* t. 2585) but the form of the divisions of the perianth is different, as well as their relative proportions. In both the flowers are of a snowy white, except the coloured marks on some of the segments.

The plant from which the accompanying figure was taken, was cultivated by Mr. Page, of Southampton, in the month of March 1832. It had been received from the Cape two years previous. It is a greenhouse plant and requires the treatment of Ixias.

The generic name is derived from *gladiolus,* a small sword, or dagger, alluding to the shape of the leaves of several of the species.

292

F.D.Smith.Del.   ACIS. rosea.   Waddell.i

ACIS ROSEA.

Rose-coloured Acis.

———

Nat. Ord. AMARYLLIDACEÆ—AMARYLLIDS of Lindley.
Linnæan Class HEXANDRIA, Order MONOGYNIA.

———

ACIS, Salisbury.—Perianth petaloid campanulate, *limb* six-parted nearly
regular, the divisions thickened at the points and just united at the
base. *Stamens* six inserted on a disk; *anthers* two-celled dehiscing
near the point. *Style* filiform; *stigma* simple obsoletely three-lobed.
Capsule three-celled. *Seeds* fleshy angulate.

———

A. rosea; leaves narrow-linear obtuse subglaucescent spreading; spathe
one-flowered; segments of the perianth oblong obtusish entire, the
margin membranaceous.

A. rosea, *Sweet in Brit. Fl. Gard.* t. 297. *Herbert Amaryllidaceæ*, 332.
Leucojum roseum, *Martius—ex Spreng. Syst.* ii. 48.
Leucojum hyemale, *Decandolle.*

———

A pretty little bulbous perennial. The bulbs are nearly
round, and produce an acute tubular membranaceous sheath,
by which the leaf and flowers are inclosed. The leaves (one
only at the time of flowering) are erect, narrowly linear, blunt,
bright green becoming somewhat glaucescent rather succulent,
slightly hollow on the upper side and convex below; after
flowering, several leaves are produced which then spread out
and remain during winter. The scapes are from one to three

232

in number flowering in succession, all single-flowered, longer than the leaves and slightly angular. The spathe is two-valved, the segments filiform acute, membranaceous, more than twice the length of the short smooth pale green pedicel. The flowers are nodding, pale rose-coloured. The perianth is campanulate, deeply six-parted, but joined at the base; its leaflets imbricate oblong entire, bluntish and terminated in a thickened point. Stamens six, inserted in the base of the perianth, on a green gland or disk; filaments very short and slender; anthers linear, opening at the point for the exclusion of the yellow pollen. Style filiform, slightly three-sided, smooth; stigma small, scarcely three-lobed. Capsule three-celled, several seeded. Seeds green fleshy, angular.

Our drawing of this delicate and elegant little species, was taken at the nursery of Messrs. Whitley, (now Osborn's), at Fulham, in the month of August, when the plants were in full bloom. The bulbs were brought by Lord Sandon from the South of Europe. The sketch of the bulb in full foliage was taken in March, several leaves having been produced after flowering, and these continued to grow until the summer. Three or four flowers are produced in succession, so that the plants continue in bloom for a considerable time.

Mr. Salisbury, in the *Paradisus Londinensis,* distinguishes those plants hitherto referred to *Leucojum,* having a filiform style, and fleshy angular seeds, by the poetic name Acis. To this genus along with *A. rosea* must be referred all the autumnal-flowering narrow-leaved species, namely *A. autumnalis, hyemalis, grandiflora,* and *trichophylla.* The true species of Leucojum are readily distinguished by their club-shaped style, and shelly seeds; they are *L. vernum, æstivum,* and *pulchellum.*

The present plant thrives in a light sandy soil, and appears to be of stronger growth than *A. autumnalis;* its bulbs too are larger, so that it is not in such danger of being lost. It must be increased by offsets from the bulbs, or by seeds, when they ripen.

Acis, whose name has been applied to these plants, was, according to the poets, a handsome Sicilian shepherd, the son of Faunus and the nymph Simæthis.

233

233

ZEPHYRANTHES *carinata*

ZEPHYRANTHES CARINATA.

Keeled-leaved Zephyr-flower.

Nat. Ord. AMARYLLIDACEÆ—AMARYLLIDS of Lindley.
Linnæan Class HEXANDRIA, Order MONOGYNIA.

ZEPHYRANTHUS, Herbert. Perianth six-parted suberect semipatent; *tube* short, narrowly funnel-shaped, alternate segments of the *limb* dissimilar; faucial membrane inconspicuous, not annular, manifested (if at all) by six very minute points above the insertion of the filaments. *Stamens* six; filaments inserted in the base of the segments, divaricate, the sepaline shorter and inserted a little lower; anthers suberect affixed below the middle. *Style* declinate; *stigma* three-lobed. *Capsule* erect, ovate, deeply three-furrowed, three-valved. *Seeds* complanate, numerous.

Z. carinata ; leaves linear acutish subfalcate longitudinally striate, obtusely keeled below; spathe tubular at the base about equal to the tube of the perianth; anthers elongate about equalling the style.

Z. carinata, *Herbert Bot. Mag.* t. 2594. *Sweet's Brit. Flow. Gard.* 2. s., t. 4.

Z. grandiflora, *Lindley Bot. Reg.* t. 992 (flower).

Amaryllis carinata, *Sprengel.*

A beautiful hardy bulb, having the bulbs oval, or turbinate with the smallest end upwards, producing many offsets. The leaves from two to four in number are from nine inches to a foot in length, linear, rather acute, more or less falcate, longitudinally striate with numerous small veins, bluntly keeled at the back, the upper side rather channelled or hollow, bright green sometimes tinged with red at the base. The scape is produced on one side, and is from four to six inches in length, hollow and slightly angular. The spathe is tubular, red, at first, dying off brown, split at the point on one side and extending the length of the tube of the flower. The flower is about two inches and a half in length, of a bright rosy lilac; the perianth divided into six segments about three parts of its length; the tube green, funnel-shaped; the segments of the limb spreading when expanded, but closing at night, elliptic acute, the three outer ones broadest and terminated with a sort of callous point, a little recurved when full blown. The stamens are six in number; their filaments inserted in the base of the segments and decurrent down the tube; the anthers are very long, about the length of the filaments, and attached to them by their back. The style is smooth, about equalling the anthers; the stigma three-lobed, papillose, the lobes fleshy, spreading, slightly recurved at the points.

This beautiful plant is quite hardy, as are most of the species of this genus. It prefers a sandy soil, and increases by the offsets. The plants from which our drawing was made were blooming in the open border in August, in the garden of Mrs. Marryatt, at Wimbledon.

The present species is a native of Mexico, and was first introduced by Mr. Bullock, who brought it with several other species from that country. It differs from *Z. grandiflora* in the shortness of its pedicel, which in that species is longer than the spathe.

The generic name is derived from *zephyros* the west wind, and *anthos* a flower, most of the species being natives of the West India islands.

234

COOPERIA pedunculata.

COOPERIA PEDUNCULATA.

Pedunculated Cooperia.

———

Nat. Ord. AMARYLLIDACEÆ.—AMARYLLIDS of Lindley.
Linnæan Class HEXANDRIA, Order MONOGYNIA.

———

COOPERIA, Herbert. Perianth six-parted erect; the *tube* very long slender cylindrical, widened at the mouth; the *limb* stellate when expanded. *Stamens* six; *filaments* inserted at the mouth, nearly equal, erect; anthers erect affixed at one-third from the base, not versatile, fasciculate. *Style* erect; *stigma* three-lobed fimbriated viscous, the lobes furrowed obtuse.

———

C. pedunculata; leaves glaucous shorter than the scape; limb of the perianth three times shorter than the tube, the segments ovate mucronate involute at the margin; capsule somewhat three-lobed.

C. pedunculata, *Herbert Amaryllidaceæ*, 179.

Zephyranthes Drummondii, *D. Don in Sweet's Brit. Flow. Gard.* 2. s., t. 328.

Sceptranthus Drummondii, *Graham, Edin. Phil. Journ.* xl. 413.

Amaryllis Drummondii, *Steudel.*

———

This pretty plant has a bulb about three inches in circumference, globose with a short neck, and clothed with a dark chocolate-brown coat. The scape is one-flowered erect, a foot high, hollow, nearly cylindrical, but slightly compressed and furrowed, glaucous green, thicker than a writing quill, bearing a cylindrical peduncle about half an inch in length, and furnished with a spathe, membranous, tubular, which is split at the top, pale-brown, and nerved, longer than the peduncle. The leaves are linear-lorate, blunt, slightly falcate, considerably shorter than the scape, glaucous, flattish, and but slightly

234

concave above, about the third of an inch broad. The perianth is funnel-shaped, white tinged with pink; the segments of its limb ovate pointed, spreading, arranged in a double series, with involute edges, the tube twice as long as the limb. There are six stamens with yellow anthers. The capsule is three-sided, almost three-lobed, having three prominent, blunt cells in which the seeds lie in two rows.

The elegant bulbous plant was gathered in Texas by the late Mr. Thomas Drummond. The accompanying drawing by Mr. James Macnab was taken from a bulb that flowered in the garden of Dr. Neill at Canonmills, near Edinburgh, in July.

The fragrant flowers of this plant as of the other species of the genus only expand fully in the evening. Dr. Herbert mentions, that in the case of the plant which he bloomed at Spofforth, "a little before sunset it expanded a little, the limb having grown pure white; in that posture it remained till the same hour the next evening when it opened a little wider, and on the third evening it made a fresh effort and reached a state of about half expansion; the next morning the sepals acquired a red tinge on the outside, and the flower began to shrivel. It had the same primrose-like fragrance of *C. Drummondiana*. The tube was quite as erect and cylindrical as in *C. Drummondiana*, the figure in *Sweet's Flower Garden*, (our t. 234), being incorrect in that respect. I was at a loss to understand the capricious non-expansion of these nocturnal flowers, but I am convinced that it arises from the manner in which they have been treated. Increase of temperature prevents their expansion. The requisite for producing a flower is a certain mean temperature, but a gradual decrease of temperature such as usually takes place at sunset, is necessary for its expansion. Therefore if the plant be in a stove or warm greenhouse and the weather cold and cloudy there is no decrease of temperature at even, but perhaps an increase on shutting the lights and making up the fire, and so circumstanced the flower of the *Cooperias* obstinately refuses to open. If placed in the open air the day before the flower is to blow, it feels the natural evening refrigeration and expands like a star, and having once attained that position it preserves it till it withers, that is, about three days."

Cooperia is named in compliment to Mr. Cooper, formerly gardener at Wentworth House, and a successful cultivator.

235.

M to U

HABRANTHUS *pratensis*

HABRANTHUS PRATENSIS.

Meadow Habranth.

———

Nat. Ord. AMARYLLIDACEÆ.—AMARYLLIDS of Lindley.
Linnæan Class HEXANDRIA, Order MONOGYNIA.

———

HABRANTHUS, Herbert. *Perianth* declined short-tubed, sub-campanulate, not convolute, more or less patent, alternate segments nearly equal; faucial membrane annular. *Stamens* six; *filaments* inserted alike at the mouth of the tube, declined, recurved semifasciculate; *anthers* affixed at the middle, incumbent, versatile. *Style* declined recurved; *stigma* three-lobed. *Capsule* turbinate.

———

H. pratensis; leaves green linear convex at the back; umbel two-three-flowered; perianth campanulate revolute at the apex, suboblique scarcely tubular; base of the filaments glandular on the outer side; faucial appendage linear-lanceolate acuminate; stigma almost simple.
H. pratensis, *Herbert Amaryllidaceæ*, 159. *Lindley in Bot. Reg.* 1842, t. 35.
Amaryllis pratensis, *Pöppig Syn.* 5.

———

A very handsome bulbous plant, having a two or three-flowered scape growing a foot or more in height, and producing broadish linear-leaves, rounded on the back, and of a green not glaucous colour. The flowers are large and showy with unequal segments, the two upper being somewhat the widest.

This beautiful plant was imported by C. B. Warner, Esq. from South Chile. It has a peculiarly brilliant appearance, on account of the contrast between the rich yellow at the

235

bottom of its flowers and bright crimson of their limb. It altogether reminds one of the Hippeastra of the warm provinces of Brazil.

"It is upon the authority of the learned Dean of Manchester," observed Dr. Lindley, (*l. c.*) "that I refer it to the *Amaryllis pratensis* of Pöppig, who says it occurs in the meadows of South Chile, near Antuco; but I have nevertheless some doubts of the identity of the plants, for the species of Pöppig is described with glaucous leaves and serrated faucial appendages, while in that before us the latter are entire and the former green. These faucial scales are unusually large in the subject of our plate, and in fact rival what occur in the curious genus *Placea*. They are of the same nature as the coronet or cup of *Narcissus*, but whether or not they also represent the thick ring on the throat of *Hippeastrum*, and the cup of *Pancratium* may be doubted."

The species prefers a light loamy soil to grow in, and sends up the flower-stems and leaves early in spring. After the flower fades, the plant ought to be grown in a light situation and freely watered, in order that it may be able to perfect its leaves. When these are fully formed and die off, it ought to be removed to a dry shelf and kept there until the period of growth comes round, when it can be watered and treated as before. Young bulbs are formed round the old one every season, by which it can be propagated.

The name *Habranthus* is derived from *habros* delicate, and *anthos* a flower; an idea very applicable to the flowers of all the species.

HABRANTHUS *miniatus*

HABRANTHUS MINIATUS.

Red Habranth.

Nat. Ord. AMARYLLIDACEÆ.—AMARYLLIDS of Lindley.
Linnæan Class HEXANDRIA, Order MONOGYNIA.

HABRANTHUS, Herbert. Perianth declined short-tubed, sub-campanulate, not convolute, more or less patent, alternate segments nearly
equal; faucial membrane annular. *Stamens* six; *filaments* inserted
alike at the mouth of the tube, declined, recurved semifasciculate;
anthers affixed at the middle, incumbent, versatile. *Style* declined
recurved; *stigma* three-lobed. *Capsule* turbinate.

H. miniatus; umbel many-flowered; perianth campanulate, the tube three
times shorter than the limb; throat bearded; scape very smooth,
scarcely taller than the leaves.
H. miniatus, *D. Don, in Sweet's Brit. Flow. Gard.* 2. s., t. 213. *Herbert's
Amaryllidaceæ,* 162.

In this pretty species the bulbs are ovate, covered with a
dark-brown membranous coat. The scape is about a foot
high, erect hollow compressed, with blunt edges, very smooth
and even, glaucous, rather thicker than a goose-quill. The
leaves are linear channelled glaucous, quite smooth, convex
and blunt underneath, with a flat rounded apex, scarcely
equalling the scape in length. The umbel is composed of
from two to five flowers, but more frequently of three, with a
spathe rather longer than the peduncles, composed of two

236

linear channelled, scariously membranous valves; the peduncles slightly compressed, smooth, an inch and a half long, intermingled with small narrow bracts. The perianth is small, red, campanulate; its limb six-parted, spreading, thrice longer than the reversely conical green tube, the throat contracted, and closed up by a white filamentose fringe; the segments lanceolate, erect, underneath paler and of a greenish cast, marked above with deeper coloured lines; the three outer segments are terminated by a green point, which is papillose at the base, and the inner ones are blunt and pointless. Stamens six, declinate, of two lengths only, the three outer ones a little shorter; filaments filiform, smooth, pale rose-colour, white at their base; anthers linear; ovary three-celled, with numerous, rounded, compressed ovules, arranged apparently in a single row. Style nearly cylindrical, longer and stouter than the filaments; stigma of three truncate, keeled, papillose, recurved lobes.

This very distinct species, well characterised by its perfectly smooth and even scape, and many-flowered spathe, is a native of Chile, and bulbs collected in that country were introduced in 1832 by Mr. Hugh Cuming. The figure was drawn at Mr. Colvill's Nursery, in July.

It requires a mixture of vegetable earth and sand, and will, doubtless, like most bulbous plants from the same country, succeed well in the open air in a warm sheltered border.

For the explanation of the generic name, see t. 235.

237

HABRANTHUS roseus.

HABRANTHUS ROSEUS.

Rose-coloured Habranth.

Nat. Ord. AMARYLLIDACEÆ.—AMARYLLIDS of Lindley.
Linnæan Class HEXANDRIA, Order MONOGYNIA.

HABRANTHUS, Herbert. Perianth declined short-tubed, sub-campanulate, not convolute, more or less patent, alternate segments nearly equal; faucial membrane annular. *Stamens* six; *filaments* inserted alike at the mouth of the tube, declined, recurved semi-fasciculate; *anthers* affixed at the middle, incumbent, versatile. *Style* declined recurved; *stigma* three-lobed. *Capsule* turbinate.

H. roseus; leaves narrow-linear, glaucous obtusish, channelled, above a foot long, two lines wide, longer than the subcompressed deeply furrowed scape; spathe one-flowered, much attenuated at the point as long as the peduncle; perianth campanulate spreading.
H. roseus, *Sweet in Brit. Flow. Gard.* 2. s. 107.

The bulbs are ovate, subpyramidal, clothed with a dark brown membranaceous scaly covering, which sheaths the leaves, nearly an inch above the bulb. The leaves are elongately and narrowly linear, bluntish at the point, glaucous, deeply channelled on the upper side, about a foot in length, and two lines broad. The scape is erect, somewhat compressed, deeply furrowed; the spathe very narrow, and tapering to a long slender point, about the length of the deeply furrowed peduncle, one-flowered. The perianth is campanulate, spreading, of a beautiful rose-colour, faintly striped with darker lines, upper segment narrow, acute, the two upper side ones broader, and the three lower ones again narrower. Stamens six, of various lengths, inserted in the mouth of the tube, two very long, and ascending at the points, two a little shorter also ascending, and two still shorter, but each pair nearly of equal lengths; anthers attached by their middle; pollen granular golden yellow; stigma trifid.

An elegant plant, native of Chiloe, whence bulbs were sent by Lieutenant Barlow to Mr. Page, nurseryman, Southampton, in whose garden the plant from which our figure was taken, flowered in June.

It will thrive well in a warm border, in the front of a stove, greenhouse, or wall; the bulbs to be covered with litter during winter, to protect them from the frost. The plant can only be increased by offsets.

The name is derived from *habros* delicate, and *anthos* a flower; the flowers of all the species being delicate in colour or texture.

W.Herbert Del.

HABRANTHUS *robustus.*

Weddell Sc.

HABRANTHUS ROBUSTUS.

Robust Habranth.

———◆———

Nat. Ord. AMARYLLIDACEÆ.—AMARYLLIDS of Lindley.
Linnæan Class HEXANDRIA, Order MONOGYNIA.

———

HABRANTHUS, Herbert. Perianth declined short-tubed, sub-campanulate, not convolute, more or less patent, alternate segments nearly equal; faucial membrane annular. *Stamens* six; *filaments* inserted alike at the mouth of the tube, declined, recurved semi-fasciculate; *anthers* affixed at the middle, incumbent, versatile. *Style* declined recurved; *stigma* three-lobed. *Capsule* turbinate.

———

H. *robustus;* scape one-flowered; spathe marcescent divided at the apex; perianth tube almost none, the faucial membrane fimbriated; leaves glaucescent.

H. robustus, *Herbert MS. in Sweet's Brit. Flow. Gard.* 2. s., t. 14.; and in *Amaryllidaceæ*, 166.

Amaryllis tubispatha, *L'Heritier*, according to Herbert.

———

A very handsome and free flowering plant having a robust scape, subglaucous channelled leaves, and a spathe undivided two-thirds of its length and a little shorter than the peduncle. The perianth is much declined, purplish pink fading to white. There is scarcely any tube; the faucial membrane is greenish fimbriated; the sepaline divisions much wider than the petals. The upper sepaline and lower petaline filaments are abridged. The flowers have a pleasant but powerful scent.

The genus may generally be recognised from *Zephyranthes* by blacker bulbs, and stiffer harder leaves.

238

This species was imported by Mr. Mackay, from the neighbourhood of Buenos Ayres. The figure was taken from a bulb which flowered at Spofforth, in July.

Sweet found it to stand the winter well, planted by the side of a wall in a border with a southern aspect, about six inches deep, an inverted garden pot being placed over it in severe frosty weather. The greatest difficulty was experienced in protecting it from slugs, which are remarkably fond of the foliage of it, as of that of *Zephyranthes candida.*

The present species flowers frequently, and at different times through the summer and autumn, and is, therefore, a very desirable plant for the flower garden. The best situation for it is at the foot of a wall, having a southern aspect, as it will not there be so liable to be injured by excess of moisture, as if grown in a more exposed situation. If the bulbs are planted about six inches deep, in a light sandy soil, they will not require the least protection, except the frost is unusually severe. If grown in pots, an equal mixture of turfy loam, peat, and sand, will be the best soil for them; and they will require the protection of frames or of the greenhouse in winter, with a good supply of water on coming into bloom; but they require very little when in a dormant state. They may be increased by offsets from the root, or by seed which will ripen in abundance if a little care be taken to fertilize the blossoms.

E.D.Smith del.

HABRANTHUS *Andersonianus*

Riddell.

HABRANTHUS ANDERSONI.

Anderson's Habranth.

Nat. Ord. AMARYLLIDACEÆ.—AMARYLLIDS of Lindley.
Linnæan Class HEXANDRIA, Order MONOGYNIA.

HABRANTHUS, Herbert. Perianth declined short-tubed, sub-campanulate, not convolute, more or less patent, alternate segments nearly
equal ; faucial membrane annular. *Stamens* six ; *filaments* inserted
alike at the mouth of the tube, declined, recurved semi-fasciculate ;
anthers affixed at the middle, incumbent, versatile. *Style* declined
recurved ; *stigma* three-lobed. *Capsule* turbinate.

H. Andersonianus ; scape one-flowered ; flowers erect ; spathe tubular,
divided at the apex, twice shorter than the peduncle ; perianth spreading,
the segments broadly ovate acute, the outer twice as broad as the
inner ; leaves linear glauceous obtusish.
H. Andersonianus, *Herbert in Bot. Reg.* t. 1345. *Sweet in Brit. Flow.
Gard.* 2. s., t. 70.

This very handsome species has round flattish bulbs. The
leaves are linear bluntish striated with faint longitudinal lines,
of a pale glaucous green. The scape is from four to six inches
in height, smooth, slightly farinose, hollow ; the spathe tubular, membranaceous, surrounding the peduncle, cleft about
one third of its length from the point ; the peduncles about
two inches long or rather more when in full bloom, cylindrical, smooth and glossy. The flowers are yellow on the inside,
239

with a handsome bright purple ring a little above the base, the outside brownish purple tinged with copper colour, variable on different plants. The perianth consists of six segments, scarcely connected at the base, longitudinally striated with numerous prominent reddish purple lines, obovately ovate spreading flat, ending in a short acute point, the outer ones about twice the size of the inner ones, closely imbricating each other. Stamens six, very variable in length. Filaments smooth, somewhat declining, about one third of the length of the segments. Anthers bursting as soon as the flowers expand. Ovary smooth and glossy, bluntly three-sided, three-celled, and three-valved, many seeded. Style smooth, a little longer than the stamens, stigma deeply three-lobed, the lobes large oblong spreading fimbriate, reflexed at the points. Seeds flat covered with a black glossy shell generally triangular, ending at the terminations in sharpish points.

Our drawing of this beautiful bulb was made in spring from a plant received from the Clapton Nursery, where in the previous September numerous bulbs of it were still in full flower in a border at the front of the greenhouse, and had continued to produce a succession of bloom the whole of the summer; the bulbs were collected at Buenos Ayres by Mr. Anderson.

The greater part of the plants from the neighbourhood of Buenos Ayres, endure our winters without any, or with very slight protection, particularly the bulbous rooted plants, as the bulbs, if planted rather deep, will be out of the reach of frost. Any that are rather tender may be covered with a mat in severe frosty weather, the mat to be removed whenever the weather is mild. The present species ripens seed in abundance, so that it may be readily increased.

HABRANTHUS *concolor*

HABRANTHUS CONCOLOR.

Whole-coloured Habranth.

Nat. Ord. AMARYLLIDACEÆ—AMARYLLIDS of Lindley.
Linnæan Class HEXANDRIA, Order MONOGYNIA.

HABRANTHUS, Herbert. Perianth declined short-tubed, sub-campanu-late, not convolute, more or less patent, alternate segments nearly equal; faucial membrane annular. *Stamens* six; *filaments* inserted alike at the mouth of the tube, declined, recurved semi-fasciculate; *anthers* affixed at the middle, incumbent, versatile. *Style* declined recurved; *stigma* three-lobed. *Capsule* turbinate.

H. concolor; leaves erect glaucescent, scape one-flowered; spathe tubular shorter than the peduncles; perianth subregular erect; sepals apiculate and as well as the petals oblong acute; faucial appendage annular lacerate.

H. concolor, *Lindley in Proc. Hort. Soc.* 1838, p. 8; *and in Bot. Reg.* 1845, t. 54.

A neat bulbous plant leafing after the flowering season. The leaves are lorate, erect, and of a bluish green. The flowers come singly on the scapes which grow about a foot high; they are erect, nearly regular, and a pale greenish yellow colour.

In the present species, the faucial appendage characteristic of Habranths consists of a membranous ring cut into irregular toothings or lacerations, and here and there slit down to the base. The flowers, although pale green, are very pretty,

240

and form a lively ornament of the greenhouse, or cold frame, in the early spring. Mr. Hartweg found it in pastures near the city of Leon in Mexico, whence he sent its bulbs to the Horticultural Society, in whose gardens the accompanying drawing was made in April 1844.

" The Habranthi in general are pretty hardy, but as their leaf should be in perfection in the winter, it must be liable to injury from frost if not protected in some manner ; they require, in order to prepare their blossom, a hot period of rest, which would be often wanting to them if exposed to our climate. When cultivated in a border, they should be covered with a glass frame, to keep them hot and dry in May, June, and July, and any covering of mats and straw that will prevent injury from severe frost may be sufficient in winter ; or they may be taken up when the leaves decay, without breaking the fibres, kept in sand, and reset three months after. As most of the bulbs are found in dry gravelly situations, they must require the border to be well drained, which should be done by a layer six inches deep of stones, covered with an inverted sod, or at least with heath, furze, or straw. The same system may be pursued with advantage in deep pots for all plants that are liable to suffer from wet, as *Habranthus Bagnoldia-nus,* and *Hesperius,* placing a thin inverted sod, or some other covering over the crocks or stones, to prevent the drainage from becoming choked, and with that precaution stronger soil may be used than would suit otherwise, and less water will be necessary." *(Herbert.)*

In the garden of the Horticultural Society this species is found to be a pretty half hardy bulb, which grows freely in a mixture of sandy loam, peat, and a small portion of well decomposed cow-dung. It is there kept dry during the autumn and winter, and in a situation free from frost at all times. It blooms in April and May, just before the leaves appear, and is increased when in a dormant state by offsets, or by seeds.

SPARAXIS. *versicolor.*

SPARAXIS VERSICOLOR.

Various-coloured Sparaxis.

———————

Nat. Ord. IRIDACEÆ—IRIDS of Lindley.
Linnæan Class TRIANDRIA, Order MONOGYNIA.

———————

SPARAXIS, Ker.—*Perianth* corolline superior, erect, spreading-funnel-shaped, tubulose, six-cleft, the tube slender short, the limb ample regular, spreading in a turbinately-stellate manner. *Stamens* adnate with the tube, included, collaterally inflexed; *anthers* linear. *Style* slender having the same direction as the stamens; *stigmas* three narrow linear, spreading recurved. *Capsule* membranaceous oblong, three-celled, three-valved, the valves bearing the septa. *Seeds* numerous in two rows, subglobose.

———————

S. versicolor; stem leafy erect branched; leaves sword-shaped, striato-nervose, uncinately mucronate; spike three or four-flowered; spathe scariose aristate, three times longer than the tube of the perianth; segments of the perianth oblong rotundate-obtuse.

S. versicolor, *Sweet in Brit. Flow. Gard.* t. 160.

———————

In this showy plant the bulb-tuber is about the size of a walnut, clothed with a netted fibrous coat. The stem is leafy, about a foot high, producing many branches, all of which terminate with a spike of flowers. The leaves are numerous, distichous, broadly ensiform, erect, pale green, or slightly glaucous, striated with numerous longitudinal veins, acute and terminated with a short slightly-hooked mucrone. The scapes are higher than the leaves, flexuose, scarcely angular,

VOL. IV.—241   H

and slightly flattened on the inner side; the spikes three or four-flowered. The spathes are two-valved, membranaceous and scariose, streaked with numerous brown and purple stripes, and terminated with several long taper-pointed segments. The perianth is funnel-shaped; its tube short and slender, about a third shorter than the scariose sheath; its limb six-parted, the segments stellately spreading when expanded, oblong and bluntly rounded, bright purple with lighter margins, and more or less clouded or diluted, marked near the base with an irregular dark spot, below which they are bright light yellow. Stamens three, inserted in the base of the limb; the filaments erect, smooth, scarcely one-third the length of the limb, joined to the back of the anthers, a little above the base; the anthers linear, the points bent inwards. The ovary is bluntly triangular; the style smooth, slender, about the length of the stamens; the stigmas three, narrowly linear, channelled, and fimbriate on the upper side, spreading, the points a little recurved.

This very beautiful plant was brought from the interior of the Cape of Good Hope, by Mr. Synnot, and flowered at the nursery of Mr. Colvill. It blooms during the summer. It is readily distinguished from *S. tricolor*, to which it is most nearly related, by its branched stem and the hooked mucro at the points of the leaves; it also produces bulbs in the axils of its leaves similar to *S. bulbifera*.

The bulbs of this species thrive best in a light sandy soil, like the other Cape bulbs to which it is related; and, like them, will succeed well planted in a bed, either in the open ground, or in a pit. If grown in the former way, the bulbs must be taken up after flowering, and laid to dry, out of the reach of frost, till the next spring; and if grown in pots, they must be treated like other Cape bulbs. They are readily increased by the offsets from the bulbs.

242

J T Hart del

SPARAIXIS. *stellaris* .

Bar

SPARAXIS STELLARIS.

Starry Sparaxis.

———

Nat. Ord. IRIDACEÆ.—IRIDS of Lindley.
Linnæan Class TRIANDRIA, Order MONOGYNIA.

———

SPARAXIS, Ker.—Perianth corolline superior, erect, spreading-funnel-shaped, tubulose, six-cleft, the tube slender short, the limb ample regular, spreading in a turbinately-stellate manner. *Stamens* adnate with the tube, included, collaterally inflexed; *anthers* linear. *Style* slender having the same direction as the stamens; *stigmas* three narrow linear, spreading, recurved. *Capsule* membranaceous oblong, three-celled, three-valved, the valves bearing the septa. *Seeds* numerous in two rows, subglobose.

———

S. stellaris; scape few-flowered, longer than the acute leaves; perianth rotately funnel-shaped, the tube filiform exserted, the segments lanceolate acute; branches of the style elongate.
S. stellaris, *D. Don in Sweet's Brit. Flow. Gard.* 2. s., t. 383.

———

This pretty species produces a round bulb-tuber, about the size of a filbert, and thickly clothed with the brown fibrous remains of past leaves. The leaves are ensiform, acute, erect, pale green, conspicuously nerved. The scapes are longer than the leaves, slightly branched and wavy, few-flowered. The spathes are cup-shaped, green, membranaceous, nerved, fringed with slender filiform, recurved ciliæ. The perianth is funnel-shaped, of a rich purple, externally rather paler; the

242

tube short filiform exserted, its mouth within of a deeper purple, and surrounded by a broad irregular starry white band; the limb turbinate, deeply six-partite, with lanceolate, pointed segments, spreading at the apex. The three stamens are shorter than the perianth, placed opposite the outer segments, and adherent to their base; their filaments filiform, glabrous, white; their anthers linear, pale yellow, longer than the free part of the filaments. The ovary is obtusely three-sided, green; the style filiform, white, thrice longer than the ovary, the branches filiform, truncate, revolute, nearly as long as the undivided portion, and minutely papillose along their upper side.

The accompanying drawing of this very pretty *Sparaxis* was taken at the nursery of Messrs. Allen and Rogers at Battersea. It comes very near to *S. tricolor* and *S. versicolor*, but is distinguished from both by the lanceolate pointed segments of its perianth, and the exserted tube. Further experience, however, must determine whether these characters are sufficient to claim for it the rank of a distinct species, for the whole of the Cape *Irideæ* vary much, both in colour and size, and very little attention has been paid to them of late years. The present species blooms in the summer months.

The present plant will require the same treatment as that recommended under t. 241 and t. 243.

For the explanation of the generic name see t. 243.

243

SPARAXIS lineata.

F.D.Smith del

Bull Lillie

SPARAXIS LINEATA.

Red-lined Sparaxis.

Nat. Ord. IRIDACEÆ.—IRIDS of Lindley.
Linnæan Class TRIANDRIA, Order MONOGYNIA.

SPARAXIS, Ker.—Perianth corolline superior, erect, spreading-funnel-shaped, tubulose, six-cleft, the tube slender short, the limb ample regular, spreading in a turbinately-stellate manner. *Stamens* adnate with the tube, included, collaterally inflexed; *anthers* linear. *Style* slender having the same direction as the stamens; *stigmas* three narrow linear, spreading, recurved. *Capsule* membranaceous oblong, three-celled, three-valved, the valves bearing the septa. *Seeds* numerous in two rows, subglobose.

S. lineata; stem erect, leafy, dichotomous; scape cylindrical glabrous, about three-flowered; leaves ensiform striate acute; spathe membranaceous with cuspidate segments; segments of the perianth erect acute, keeled beneath.

S. lineata, *Sweet in Brit. Flow. Gard.* 2. s., t. 131.

The bulb-tubers of this species are clothed with a reticulated fibrous net-work, composed of the bases of the former leaves. The leaves are distichous, ensiform, acute, oblique from about the middle, about half an inch in breadth, and from five to eight inches in length. The flower-stem is erect, leafy below, frequently forked, the scapes two to four-flowered, cylindrical, smooth; the spathe scarcely an inch long, two-valved, its valves ovate, lacerate at the point, veined with

243

chestnut-coloured veins, and ending in slender points. The perianth is six-parted; the tube about three lines long, its throat yellow; the segments six, erect, tapering to the base, acute, keeled at the back, longitudinally marked with a red line, and more or less tinged with pink; on the inside they are yellow at the base, marked about the middle with a brown mark, the upper part white. Stamens three, the filaments dilated below to about the middle. The style is smooth, scarcely half the length of the limb. The stigmas are three in number, slender, spreading, dilated at the points, and fimbriate.

Our drawing of this pretty species of Sparaxis, was taken from a bulb at the nursery of the late Mr. Colvill, of Chelsea. It flowers in the spring; and is a very pretty neat plant, and apparently a very free bloomer.

The plant that produced the specimen here figured had only a simple scape, which was, most probably, the reason of its bearing four flowers; they more frequently produce a forked scape, with three flowers on the middle one, and two on the side one.

The bulbs may be grown in a pit, covered with a mat in winter. All the Cape, Mexican, and Chilian bulbs, however, succeed quite as well in a warm dry border, in a mixture of sandy loam and peat, and to be covered with a mat in very wet or sharp frosty weather; or the bulbs may be taken up after flowering, and if kept in a cool dry place they may be kept out of the ground till early in spring, when all the sharp frost is over.

The generic name is derived from the Greek *sparazo*, from its torn or lacerated spathes.

Smith. Del.   OVIEDA *ancops.*   Weddell sc.

OVIEDA ANCEPS.

Flat-stemmed Ovieda.

———

Nat. Ord. IRIDACEÆ.—IRIDS of Lindley.
Linnæan Class TRIANDRIA, Order MONOGYNIA.

———

OVIEDA, Sprengel.—*Perianth* corolline superior funnel-shaped; tube filiform-triquetrous, constricted at the throat; limb six-parted erect or
spreading, the segments equal. *Stamens* three, inserted in the throat
of the perianth, erect or subsecund; *filaments* subulate; *anthers* oblong
affixed by the base. *Ovary* inferior triquetrous three-celled; *ovules*
many, in two rows in the central angle of the cells, adscendent, anatropous. *Style* filiform; *stigmas* three, narrow linear conduplicate two-
parted, lobes revolute. *Capsule* membranaceous three-lobed triquetrous,
three-celled, loculicidally three-valved.

———

O. anceps; scape leafy, subtriquetrously two-edged, branched; leaves
sword-shaped crisped at the edges; spathes leafy crisply toothed;
segments of the perianth spathulate concave.
O. anceps *Sprengel, Syst. Veg.* i. 147.
Lapeyrousia anceps, *Ker, Ann. Bot.* i. 238. *Sweet's Brit. Flow. Gard.,*
t. 143.
Lapeyrousia compressa, *Pourret, Act. Tol.* iii. 39.
Gladiolus anceps, *Vahl, Enum.* ii. 108.

———

In this pretty plant the bulb is small, about the size of a
large marrowfat pea, clothed with a hard glossy brown shell.
The stem is about a span high, branched, flat; the main stem
three-edged, the side ones flat and two-edged; all the edges
toothed with numerous small teeth. The leaves are broadly
ensiform, many-nerved, short and blunt, the edges more or
less curled, and sometimes toothed, rather glaucous or light

244

green ; the upper ones or spathes are very short, sheathing the stem ; and inside of the outer valve is a membranaceous sheath with two leafy toothed edges, terminated in a bifid point, and enclosing the bottom of the tube. The perianth has a long slender tube of a bluish purple ; and a hypocrateriform limb divided into six segments, which are spathulately-lanceolate, the points slightly curved inwards ; two upper segments are rather the largest, dark blue light at the sides near the base ; the others narrower keeled at the back and the white sides near the base larger and stronger. Stamens three, distinct, inserted in the upper part of the tube ; the filaments smooth, attached to the back of the anthers; the anthers sagittate. The style smooth, long and slender, exserted ; the stigmas three, of a blue purple, each two-parted and fimbriate, the points curling or twisted irregularly.

This very pretty plant was first introduced to our gardens from the Cape by Mr. Synnot. It flowered in the collection of the late Mr. Colvill.

These plants will succeed well if planted out about the latter end of March, or beginning of April, in a bed of prepared soil raised a little in the centre and gradually falling to each side, that the moisture may pass off, without injuring the bulbs. The soil should be sandy and light. The plant being of low growth, it should be planted in one of the front rows, and not more than three inches deep, for the bulb being small, it would be liable to rot if planted deep. As soon as it has done flowering, and the stalks are decayed, it may be taken up and kept in a dry place, where no frost can get at it, till the following spring, when the bed must be made up afresh, and some fresh mould and sand must be added. If left in the ground all the winter, it will require covering in sharp frost, or very wet weather. If grown in pots in frames or in the greenhouse, a mixture of loam, peat, and sand, is the best soil for it. Seeds ripen freely, if some pollen be brushed on the stigmas when in bloom.

OVIEDA aculeata

OVIEDA ACULEATA.

Prickly-stemmed Ovieda.

———◆———

Nat. Ord. IRIDACEÆ.—IRIDS of Lindley.
Linnæan Class TRIANDRIA, Order MONOGYNIA.

———

OVIEDA, Sprengel.—*Perianth* corolline superior funnel-shaped; tube filiform-triquetrous, constricted at the throat; limb six-parted erect or spreading, the segments equal. *Stamens* three, inserted in the throat of the perianth, erect or subsecund; *filaments* subulate; *anthers* oblong affixed by the base. *Ovary* inferior triquetrous three-celled; *ovules* many, in two rows in the central angle of the cells, adscendent, anatropous. *Style* filiform; *stigmas* three, narrow linear conduplicate two-parted, lobes revolute. *Capsule* membranaceous three-lobed-triquetrous, three-celled, loculicidally three-valved.

———

O. aculeata; scape leafy branched, the branches two-edged compressed, aculeately toothed; root leaves sword-shaped acute plaited, those of the stem shorter broader bluntish, with curled margins; spathe leafy curled twice shorter than the perianth tube; segments of the perianth oblong spreading, the lower ones appendiculate at the base.
O. aculeata.
Lapeyrousia aculeata, *Sweet Hort. Brit.* 896.
Peyrousia aculeata, *Sweet Brit. Flow. Gard.* 2. s., t. 39.

———

The bulb in this species is small, similar to that of *O. anceps.* The leaves are plaited, smooth; those at the root, lanceolate ensiform, acute, not unlike the leaflets of a plaited palm, the margins smooth, not curled; those on the scape much shorter and broader, the lower ones nearly ovate, bluntish, with curled margins, upper ones longer, narrower and more acute, also with curled edges. The scape is about a span high, branching, the branches all with two flat winged edges, thickly clothed with innocuous prickle-like teeth, which are more numerous and longer than in *O. anceps*. The spathe is two-valved; the outer valve leaf-like, acute with much curled edges, scarcely half the length of the tube of the flower; the inner valve not half the length of the outer, membranaceous, acute, with two strong leafy green nerves, which are also aculeate. The flowers are alternate, rather distant, sessile, white. The perianth with a long slender tube, more than double the length of the sheath, inflated towards the mouth; the limb six-cleft, its segments spreading flat, the three upper ones oblong, bluntish or scarcely acute, about double the size of the lower ones, narrower at the base, the lower ones more acute, the points slightly curved inwards, all marked near the bend with a red spot, which is darker in the middle one, than in the others; the lower segments, a little below the bend, have a prominent hooked tooth winged at the bottom with red margins, and not unlike barren filaments. There are three stamens inserted in the throat, the filaments smooth, attached to the back of the anthers, the anthers linear, sagittate at the base, purple. Ovary smooth, bluntly three-sided; style smooth, about the height of the stamens, a little exserted; stigmas three, bifid, spreading, fimbriate, the points of the segments again slightly cloven.

This very curious and pretty plant, is a native of the Cape of Good Hope, from whence it was brought to this country by Mr. Synnot. The Cape bulbs are highly interesting though not now fashionable, and therefore neglected. If a little pains however was taken with them, to grow them in beds in the open air, we should have them in great perfection, and nothing can produce a more elegant and pleasing an appearance, than a bed of the different genera and species of this tribe. The best soil for them is an equal quantity of light turfy loam, peat, and sand, or if peat cannot be easily procured, decayed leaves or very rotten dung that has been well exposed and dried in the sun will answer the same purpose, so that it be quite free from caterpillars, or other insects. The soil must be quite light, that the shoots may come readily through it. The bulbs may either be taken up after flowering, and kept dry till the end of October, or if the ground should not become too hard, they may continue in the same situation, requiring nothing but the covering of a mat or some sort of litter in severe frost. They may be increased by offsets from the root, or by seed.

E.D.Smith.Del.   SYNNOTIA. variegata.   Weddell Sc.

SYNNOTIA VARIEGATA.

Variegated-flowered Synnotia.

Nat. Ord. IRIDACEÆ.—IRIDS of Lindley.
Linnæan Class TRIANDRIA, Order MONOGYNIA.

SYNNOTIA, Sweet.—Perianth corolline, tubulose, six-parted, sub-two-lipped, gaping. *Spathes* two-valved, membranaceous, torn. *Stamens* three adscendent, inserted in the base of the limb. *Stigmas* three, dilated at the apex fimbriate, recurved-spreading. *Capsule* oblong three-cornered. *Seeds* globose shining.

S. variegata ; leaves sword-shaped acute oblique at the base, two ranked ; scape somewhat branched about as long as the leaves; upper segments of the perianth elliptic erect, the two lateral oblong recurved at the points, the three lower spathulate concave, bent backwards.
S. variegata *Sweet in Brit. Flow. Gard.* t. 150.

The bulb-tuber of this plant is about the size and shape of a small walnut, clothed with a hard reticulately fibrous whitish shell. The leaves are flat, ensiform oblique towards the base, acute, striated with numerous small lines, sheathing at the base, about the length of the scape, the upper ones sometimes undulate or curled near the margins, of a pale green colour. The scape sometimes simple, and sometimes producing a branch or two, the lower part a little flattened, upper part nearly cylindrical, slightly glaucous. The spathes are two-valved, membranaceous, striate, much torn at the

246

points, the segments long and taper-pointed. The flower from three to five on each branch, are sessile—the perianth ringent, two-lipped, with a long slender tube, the limb leaning forward; the tube pale, tinged with purple; the limb campanulate at the base, deeply six-parted, and marked inside, below the segments, with six elegant dark blue stripes; the upper segment is elliptic, bluntish, erect or slightly twisted, of a beautiful dark blue, tinged with purple; the two side ones are oblong, blunt, slightly reflexed, of the same colour; the three lower ones spathulate, narrow at the base, reflexed about the middle where the sides fold inwards, and the points are bent downwards, while from near the point to the base is a large white, or sulphur-coloured mark, edged with dark blue. Stamens three, distinct, joined to the base of the limb; filaments smooth, nearly straight or slightly ascending, joined to the back of the anthers, which are linear and sagittate at the base; pollen purple. Style long and slender, smooth; stigmas three, spreading, simple, the points widened and fimbriate, slightly recurved.

This very handsome and free flowering plant is one of the curious bulbs brought from the interior of the Cape, by Mr. W. Synnot. Sweet considered it, with other irregular flowered species that had been referred to *Sparaxis*, to form a distinct genus, which he named in compliment to the gentleman who introduced it. "The genus" he says "is readily distinguished from *Sparaxis* by its long slender tube and irregular limb. Our drawing was made at the late Mr. Colvill's Nursery, in the month of September.

The bulbs of this natural order, may be planted either in beds in the open ground, in borders by the side of a south wall, or in a pit made on purpose to be covered with lights in winter. If planted in beds in the open garden, they must be composed of a light sandy soil, or a mixture of light turfy loam, peat, and sand, chopped up well and mixed together, will suit them very well, the beds being made to slope on each side, to carry off the moisture; if the bulbs are dry, they may be planted in the same manner as Tulips, but if growing in pots, the balls should be turned into the ground without breaking them.

ANISANTHUS *splendens*

ANISANTHUS SPLENDENS.

Splendid Anisanthus.

Nat. Ord. IRIDACEÆ.—IRIDS of Lindley.
Linnæan Class TRIANDRIA, Order MONOGYNIA.

ANISANTHUS, Sweet.—Perianth corolline, tubulose, the tube slender at the base, triangularly gibbous about the middle, one lipped; the limb unequal six-parted gaping, the upper segment very long spoon-shaped, the side ones bent upwards, the three lower ones small. *Stamens* three, adscendent. *Stigmas* three, spreading, cuneate-ligulate, entire, dilated at the apex. *Capsule* triangularly oblong, three-valved. *Seeds* numerous in two rows, winged.

A. splendens; scape simple erect; leaves linear sword-shaped acute glabrous nervose, flowers distichous; upper segment of perianth galeate channelled above; spathes acute subequal; stigmas cuneate fringed.
A. splendens, *Sweet in Hort. Brit. ed.* 2. 500; and in *Brit. Flow. Gard.* 2. s., t. 84.
Antholyza splendens, *Steudel Nom. Bot.* 106.

This showy plant has bulb-tubers about the size of a large hazel nut, clothed with a hard dark brown shell. The stem is from two to three feet high, purple at the base. The leaves are long erect linear or linearly ensiform, acute, smooth, strongly two or three nerved, with smaller nerves intermixed, oblique at the base. The scape is simple, leafy nearly cylindrical, and glaucous. The spike is distichous, many-flowered, the flowers spreading out on each side. The spathe two-valved; the valves being about equal in length, lanceolate, acute, glaucous, reaching to the bottom of the limb. The perianth is tubular, one-lipped; the tube slender at the base, triangularly gibbous about the middle; the limb six-parted, the upper segment spoon-shaped with a long claw, rounded at the point, and channelled above, leaning forward like a helmet, of a bright scarlet; the side ones are also unguiculate, spreading and ascending, the unguis membranaceously margined, from the bend ovate, blunt, also bright scarlet; the

247

three lower ones are small, yellowish green, the side ones very small, lanceolate, acute, rigid, the points bent inwards, the middle one broadly spathulate, the rounded point reflexed, and sometimes tipped with scarlet. Stamens three, ascending, inserted in the middle of the gibbous part of the tube; the filaments smooth, attached to the middle of the back of the anthers; the anthers slightly sagittate at the base, with golden yellow pollen. The ovary is oblong, triangular; the style smooth, about the length of the stamens; the stigmas three, spreading, dilated at the points, and slightly fimbriate. The numerous seeds are winged.

This beautiful and splendid bulb was introduced from the Cape of Good Hope by Mr. Synnot in 1825, and was bloomed by the late Mr. Colvill, in his nursery at Chelsea, where our drawing was made. The bulbs flower in March and April, and attain the height of from two to three feet, the spike of flowers being nearly a foot in length. It differs from *A. Cunonius*, in the much broader and more nerved leaves; in the flowers being all distichous, instead of secund, in the nearly equal length of the valves of the spathe, which are very unequal in *A. Cunonius*, and also in its much greater
e.

Sweet separated the present genus from *Gladiolus* and *Antholyza*, on account of its habit and character being very different from both; and he considered the unequal segments of the flowers to distinguish it from *Gladiolus*; as do the flat winged seeds from *Antholyza*.

The bulbs of the present species should be potted in a mixture of nearly half light turfy loam, one fourth of fine white sand, and the rest peat, in which they thrive or they may be planted out in a pit, where all the Cape bulbs succeed with a little covering in winter. They will also succeed well in a warm border in the open ground, but will then require the protection of a mat, or some other covering, in frosty weather, or during a continuance of rain, but to be always exposed when the weather will permit. They may, by perseverance, be made to remain dormant in winter, and to be planted out in spring, and will then require but little care. They may be increased by offsets from the bulbs, and by seeds.

The generic name is derived from *anisos*, unequal, and *anthos*, a flower, from the inequality of the segments of the flower.

ANISANTHUS *Planch.*

ANISANTHUS PLANTII.

Plant's Anisanth.

———

Nat. Ord. IRIDACEÆ.—IRIDS of Lindley.
Linnæan Class TRIANDRIA, Order MONOGYNIA.

ANISANTHUS, Sweet.—Perianth corolline, tubulose, the tube slender at the base, triangularly gibbous about the middle, one lipped ; the limb unequal six-parted gaping, the upper segment very long, spoon-shaped, the side ones bent upwards, the three lower ones small. *Stamens* three, adscendent. *Stigmas* three, spreading, cuneate-ligulate, entire, dilated at the apex. *Capsule* triangularly oblong, three valved. *Seeds* numerous cumulate in two rows, winged.

A. Plantii ; scape erect, simple ; leaves linear sword-shaped acute, strongly nerved ; flowers distichous ; upper segments with involute margins, the central one slightly longer, the lateral ones spreading ; lower segments equal ; spathes obtuse unequal ; stigmas capitate fringed.
A. Plantii.
A. splendens, var. hybridus, *London Hot. Brit.*
Plant's Anisanth, *Bot. Reg.* 1842, t. 53.

This very beautiful bulb is of vigorous erect growth, the stem furnished with long narrow sword-shaped leaves, and the flowers crowded in a distichous arrangement, on a long upright spike. They are rich scarlet, the three upper segments several times longer than the lower, and themselves nearly equal in size, the side ones spreading, not ascending ; the three small lower segments are equal in size, red with pale margins. The spathes are blunt and very unequal, with pallid edges. The three arms of the style are terminated by capitate fringed stigmas.

This beautiful plant is a mule obtained by Mr. Plant, nurseryman, Cheadle, from whom the specimen here figured were received by Dr. Lindley in September, 1841, accompanied by the following note :—

" It originated here, and bloomed for the first time in 1838. It is the produce of seed from *Anisanthus splendens*

248

and *Gladiolus Colvillii*, the latter, itself a hybrid. The present one is, as far as my humble abilities will allow me to judge, exactly intermediate, being entirely wanting in that peculiar mode of increase which obtains in *Anisanthus splendens*—1 mean by means of tubers, or in the manner of potatoes—a fact which Sweet has taken no notice of in establishing the genus *Anisanthus*. In the practice of hybridizing we know but little yet. Would you believe that I have some seedlings between *Gladiolus* and *Amaryllis?* I have this day taken the roots up, some of which present a most curious appearance; neither bulbs nor scales, but something of both."

"Here," observes Dr. Lindley, " is not only a fine addition to flowering plants, but abundant subject for consideration. In the first place we have a mule between two different genera; for, although the Anisanths and Corn-Flags are only distinguished by the extreme obliquity of the flower of the former and their peculiar mode of propagation, and are consequently regarded by many Botanists as separated upon insufficient grounds, yet it must be confessed that their differences are fully as great as in other cases are admitted as good marks of genera. But supposing the Anisanths and Corn-Flags to be of the same genus, at least there is this remarkable in the history of this plant, that one of its parents is itself a mule. What, however, are we to say of Mr. Plant's observation as to his having crossed the Corn-Flag and Amaryllis? We should once have thought such a thing impossible, but every day is bringing forward such startling facts regarding vegetable fertilization, that for our own parts we are prepared to expect a cross between an Oak and a Spanish Chesnut, or any other seemingly impossible production."

Anisanthus Plantii is a greenhouse, bulbous plant, requiring the same treatment as Antholyzas, Cape Gladioli, or Ixias. It thrives best when potted in a mixture of sandy loam, leaf-mould, and a little peat. The bulbs should be potted about October, and set in a cool close frame (where they are secure from mice and frost), till they have filled the pots with roots; afterwards they should be removed to a warmer situation to flower. After they have done flowering, they should be gradually rested by withholding water, and finally the roots should be removed from the soil, which is much better and safer than to allow them to remain in the pots, for they always start much better the next season.

IRIS

IRIS SWERTII.

Swert's Flower de luce.

———

Nat. Ord. IRIDACEÆ.—IRIDS of Lindley.
Linnæan Class TRIANDRIA, Order MONOGYNIA.

IRIS, *Linnæus.*—*Perianth* corolline, superior; tube short; limb six-parted, the exterior segments most often reflexed, bearded or rarely naked at the base, the interior erect often smaller or minute. *Stamens* three, inserted at the base of the outer segments of the perianth; *filaments* filiform or subulate; *anthers* oblong, affixed by the base. *Ovary* inferior, obsoletely three-cornered, three-celled; *ovules* numerous, horizontal, anatropous, in two rows in the central angle of the cells. *Style* triquetrous, the base often connate with the tube; *stigmas* three, petaloid-dilated, keeled above, channelled beneath, rarely two-lipped, opposite the stamens. *Capsule* coriaceous, trigonal or hexagonal, three-celled, loculicidally three-valved at the apex. *Seeds* numerous, plano-compressed, marginate.

I. *Swertii;* bearded; stem many-flowered, terete, taller than the leaves; segments of the perianth replicate-undulate, the exterior recurvate oblong-spathulate emarginate, the interior roundish-oval larger.
I. Swertii, *Lam. Dict.* iii, 296. *Sweet's Brit. Flow. Gard.* 2. s., 254.
I. portugalensis, *Besl. Hort. Eystett.* i., t. 6.

A very pretty perennial of which the whole herbage is of a glaucous hue. The rhizome is thick, and fragrant. The stem erect, round, from a foot to eighteen inches high, bearing about three flowers, and rather longer than the leaves, which are broadly ensiform, slightly falcate, an inch or more in width. The flowers are sessile, or nearly so, about half the size of *I. germanica*, white, marked, especially at the borders, with numerous contiguous transverse streaks, of a pale purple or violet. The spathes are oblong-lanceolate acute, thin and scariose, white, as long as the tube of the perianth, which is angular, green marked with purple lines, and about the length of the ovary. The outer segments of the perianth are oblong-spathulate, recurved and spreading, plaited and waved at the border, slightly notched at the top, furnished at the claw with copious, erect, white hairs, tipped with yellow; the three inner segments are broadly elliptical, with a contracted claw, the edges more wavy and recurved. The filaments of the stamens are blue; the anthers linear-oblong, pale yellow. The ovary is oblong, with three blunt angles; the stigmas violet, cloven, with pointed entire lobes, the outer lip very short, truncate, emarginate and slightly revolute.

This very elegant *Iris* has been long cultivated in the gardens, but of its origin and native country nothing certain is known. It is very nearly related to *I. germanica*, from which it is chiefly distinguished by the smaller size of all its parts, and by the narrower and wavy segments of its perianth. We have not remarked whether the flowers are fragrant.

Mr. Bellenden Ker proposed to combine this plant with *I. plicata* and *nudicaulis*, under the name of *I. aphylla*; in which view we are disposed to concur. Mr. Swainson, after devoting considerable attention to the study of this genus, recognized three distinct types or forms, the European, Asiatic, and American, which, with few exceptions, appear to be natural.

Our drawing was taken from a specimen that blossomed at Mr. Knight's nursery, in May,

This plant is a hardy perennial, requiring only to be planted in moderately good garden earth. Like other Irises it increases readily by division.

IRIS *hungarica.*

IRIS HUNGARICA.

Hungarian Flower de luce.

———◆———

Nat. Ord. IRIDACEÆ.—IRIDS of Lindley.
Linnæan Class TRIANDRIA, Order MONOGYNIA.

IRIS, Linnæus.—Perianth corolline, superior; tube short; limb six-parted; the exterior segments most often reflexed, bearded or rarely naked at the base, the interior erect often smaller or minute. *Stamens* three, inserted at the base of the outer segments of the perianth; *filaments* filiform or subulate; *anthers* oblong, affixed by the base. *Ovary* inferior, obsoletely three-cornered, three-celled; *ovules* numerous, horizontal, anatropous, in two rows in the central angle of the cells. *Style* triquetrous, the base often connate with the tube; *stigmas* three, petaloid-dilated, keeled above, channelled beneath, rarely two-lipped, opposite the stamens. *Capsule* coriaceous, trigonal or hexagonal, three-celled, loculicidally three-valved at the apex. *Seeds* numerous, plano-compressed, marginate.

I. hungarica; bearded; leaves ensiform glabrous subfalcate, nearly equalling the many-flowered scape : spathe inflated; the upper two-flowered.
 I. hungarica, *Waldsten and Kitaibel Hung.* iii, 226; *Sweet's Brit. Flower Gard.* t. 74.

This fine species has large, tuberous rhizomes. The leaves are ensiform smooth generally falcate, nerved with numerous prominent nerves, taper-pointed, about equal with the many-flowered scape. The spathes are inflated; sheaths two, opposite acute, keeled, inclosing the peduncle germen and tube.
 250

The perianth is six-parted, of a beautiful blue purple; its tube an inch in length, bluntly trigonal, trisulcate, smooth and glossy; the outer segments narrowest, reflexed, densely bearded from the base to above the middle, and variegated near the base; the inner ones broadly obovate, erect, connivent or closing towards each other at the points, also variegated near the base. Stamens three, inserted in the base of the segments, about half the length of the stigmas; filaments flat, smooth; anthers linear, attached to the filament a little above the base, nearly as long as the filaments, and bearing white pollen. The style is short, acutely three-cornered; the stigmas three, petal-like, keeled inwards, the points deeply cloven, acute and jagged at the sides.

This fine species of Iris is a native of Hungary, and is readily distinguished from most others by its falcate leaves. Our drawing was taken from a plant at the nursery of the late Mr. Colvill, in May.

It is quite hardy, and thrives well in a rich light soil, flowering in May and June, and sometimes again in autumn. It is not one of the strongest growing sorts, but is of middle stature, the leaves seldom exceeding a foot in height, and the flower stems are not so high, but the flowers are large, and very showy, and several are expanded at the same time. The best method of increasing it, is by dividing the roots, but it may be also raised from seeds, which sometimes ripen; these should be sown as soon as ripe, either in pots, or in the open ground, transplanting them quite young, that they may not suffer from removal.

IRIS

IRIS BIFLORA.

Two-flowered Flower de luce.

Nat. Ord. IRIDACEÆ.—IRIDS of Lindley.
Linnæan Class TRIANDRIA, Order MONOGYNIA.

IRIS, Linnæus.—*Perianth* corolline, superior; tube short; limb six-parted, the exterior segments most often reflexed, bearded or rarely naked at the base, the interior erect often smaller or minute. *Stamens* three, inserted at the base of the outer segments of the perianth; *filaments* filiform or subulate; *anthers* oblong, affixed by the base. *Ovary* inferior, obsoletely three-cornered, three-celled; *ovules* numerous, horizontal, anatropous, in two rows in the central angle of the cells. *Style* triquetrous, the base often connate with the tube; *stigmas* three, petaloid-dilated, keeled above, channelled beneath, rarely two-lipped, opposite the stamens. *Capsule* coriaceous, trigonal or hexagonal, three-celled, loculicidally three-valved at the apex. *Seeds* numerous, plano-compressed, marginate.

I. biflora; scape slightly pruinose with short foliaceous spathes; radical leaves ensiform falcate acute striated; segments of the perianth oblong-ovate entire undulate attenuated at the base, the interior inflexed, the exterior reflexed; tube twice the length of the ovary.

I. biflora, *Linn. Syst. Veg.* 90. *Sweet's Brit. Flow. Gard.* 2. s., t. 152.

I. bohemica, *Schmidt Fl. Bohem.* 303.

The root of the present species is perennial, tuberous, spreading considerably and branching. The leaves generally five on the leaf-shoots in the flowering season, are more or less falcate, some of them very much so, the longest ten inches

251

and a half in length, the broadest about an inch in breadth, gradually becoming smaller downwards, glaucous and very strongly striated. The scape is two or three-flowered, clothed with short spathaceous leaves, which scarcely reach from one joint to the next. The spathe is two-leaved clasping the peduncle, ovary, and part of the tube, green, more or less marked with violet. The flowers are a purple violet, on peduncles longer than the ovary, which is very short, about half the length of the tube, six-lined, at first cylindrical, but soon becoming three-sided. The tube of the perianth is green tinged with blue upwards, obtusely angular; the three outer segments ovately obovate, rounded at the points, undulate, tapering to the base, from the base to the bend and a little above striped with white, from the base to the middle clothed with a close line of white hairs tipped with violet, and towards the end nearly altogether violet; the three inner segments are erect or bent a little inwards at the top, considerably broader than the outer ones, much more undulated and crumpled, notched at the point, ovately oval, very much attenuated at the base, the margins curved inwards, pale brown striped with a darker brown. Stamens three; filaments flat and tapering upwards; anthers linear. Style short, triangular, stigma deeply three-parted, the segments petal-like, rather larger than usual, elliptic, keeled on the upper side and hollow below, the lacerate points split down to the membrane.

Our drawing was taken at the Apothecaries' Garden at Chelsea, in May, the plant continuing to produce a quantity of flower scapes, from the beginning of April till the middle of May. Mr. Anderson first introduced it in the year 1826.

The present species is a native of Portugal, it also appears to be from Bohemia and Russia. It requires the ordinary herbaceous plant culture.

252.

IRIS *imbricata*

IRIS IMBRICATA.

Imbricated Flower de luce.

Nat. Ord. IRIDACEÆ.—IRIDS of Lindley.
Linnæan Class TRIANDRIA, Order MONOGYNIA.

IRIS, Linnæus,—Perianth corolline, superior; tube short; limb six-parted, the exterior segments most often reflexed, bearded or rarely naked at the base, the interior erect often smaller or minute. *Stamens* three, inserted at the base of the outer segments of the perianth; *filaments* filiform or subulate; *anthers* oblong, affixed by the base. *Ovary* inferior, obsoletely three-cornered, three-celled; *ovules* numerous, horizontal, anatropous, in two rows in the central angle of the cells. *Style* triquetrous, the base often connate with the tube; *stigmas* three, petaloid-dilated, keeled above, channelled beneath, rarely two-lipped, opposite the stamens. *Capsule* coriaceous, trigonal or hexagonal, three-celled, loculicidally three-valved at the apex. *Seeds* numerous, plano-compressed, marginate.

I. imbricata; leaves broad rigid erect, shorter than the somewhat branched scape; bracts ovate obtuse distichous foliaceous membranaceous at the apex, imbricate; sepals bearded rounded at the apex, petals obovate emarginate; tube very short.

I. imbricata, *Lindley in Bot. Reg.* 1845, t. 35.

This is a very showy perennial with the habit of the larger rhizomatous Irises. The leaves are broad rigid and erect. The scape is somewhat branched, longer than the leaves, and bearing in a distichous arrangement ovate-obtuse foliaceous bracts, which are membranaceous at the apex, and closely imbricate.

The flowers are pale yellow, and have a very short tube which is enclosed by the bracts; the outer segments of the perianth are bearded, and rounded at the points, the inner obovate and emarginate.

The specimens from which the accompanying figure was made were forwarded in May, 1844, from Spofforth, by the Hon. and Very Rev. the Dean of Manchester.

With the history of the plant we are unacquainted. Dr. Lindley thought it probably a mere variety of *I. squalens*; from which, as he points out, it differs in its pure lemon-coloured flowers, and in the imbricated short blunt convex bracts which invest their base. Spach on the other hand, unites it with *I. flavescens*, from which its sheathing bracts and the short tube of its perianth seem to distinguish it. It is probably entitled to specific rank.

At any rate it is a very showy perennial, which proves quite hardy in the open border, and grows freely if planted in a rich sandy loam and warm situation. It is increased by dividing the old plants any time from October to March, and flowers about the end of May.

258

IRIS *flavescens*

IRIS FLAVESCENS.

Pale yellow Flower de luce.

———

Nat. Ord. IRIDACEÆ.—IRIDS of Lindley.
Linnæan Class TRIANDRIA, Order MONOGYNIA.

———

IRIS, Linnæus.—Perianth corolline, superior ; tube short ; limb six-parted, the exterior segments most often reflexed, bearded or rarely naked at the base, the interior erect often smaller or minute. *Stamens* three, inserted at the base of the outer segments of the perianth ; *filaments* filiform or subulate ; *anthers* oblong, affixed by the base. *Ovary* inferior, obsoletely three-cornered, three-celled ; *ovules* numerous, horizontal, anatropous, in two rows in the central angle of the cells. *Style* triquetrous, the base often connate with the tube ; *stigmas* three, petaloid-dilated, keeled above, channelled beneath, rarely two-lipped, opposite the stamens. *Capsule* coriaceous, trigonal or hexagonal, three-celled, loculicidally three-valved at the apex. *Seeds* numerous, plano-compressed, marginate.

———

I. flavescens ; bearded ; leaves lanceolate acute somewhat plicate, half-shorter than the branched stem ; lower spathes subfoliaceous, upper membranaceous ; outer segments of the perianth reflexed, interior obovate with long hairs within at the base ; tube as long as the six-furrowed ovary.
   I. flavescens, *Redouté, Liliaceæ,* vii. t. 375. *Sweet's Brit. Flow. Gard.* 2. s, f. 56.

———

In this species the rhizome is tuberous, and knotted. The stem grows about two feet high, and is smooth nearly twice the length of the leaves, generally from four to six-flowered, leafy towards the base, naked from below the middle upwards. The leaves are distichous, somewhat plaited, or strongly nerved so as to occasion a plaited appearance, and somewhat glaucous, straight or occasionally a little twisted : the lower ones sword-shaped ending in a sharp point, the stem-ones shorter, somewhat falcate, lanceolate, clasping the stem at their base. The bracts are membranaceous, the length of the tube, the lower one leaf-like, with membranaceous point and margins, the upper ones thin and membranaceous. The flowers are sessile, of a pale yellow ; the tube green, slightly triangular, about the length of or a little longer than the ovary ; the limb spreading, its three outer segments broadly obovate, rounded at the points, becoming gradually slenderer downwards, bearded with bright yellow hairs about half way up, and marked with numerous branching brown veins from the base to about half way up, becoming paler upwards, at first flat and spreading, afterwards reflexed from about the middle ; its three inner segments erect, the points bent inwards a little, obovate, very much attenuated at the base, where the sides close inwards, and enclose a tuft of long yellow hairs. The three stamens are inserted in the tube, and have linear anthers bearing white granular pollen. The ovary is sessile, oblong, six-channelled, smooth ; the style acutely triangular ; the stigmas three, petal-like, spreading, pale bright yellow, oblong, slightly attenuated to the base, sharply keeled on the upper side, and concave or hollow underneath, where they cover and hide the stamens, deeply cleft into two segments which are spreading, ovate, attenuated at the points, entire on the inner side, but deeply and sharply serrated on the outer sides, entire below the segments.

Our drawing of this pretty species was taken in May from a plant that flowered in the garden of the Apothecaries Company at Chelsea. Mr. Anderson had received it under the name of *I. lutéscens*.

It is not precisely known, of what country the present plant is a native, but Redoute states it to be cultivated in the gardens of Paris ; and it is supposed to be from Switzerland.

It thrives well in the common garden soil, and flowers in May and the beginning of June, and is readily increased by dividing at the root.

254

IRIS SETOSA.

Bristle-tipped Flower de luce.

———◆———

Nat. Ord. IRIDACEÆ.—IRIDS of Lindley.
Linnæan Class TRIANDRIA, Order MONOGYNIA.

———————

IRIS, Linnæus.—Perianth corolline, superior; tube short; limb six-parted, the exterior segments most often reflexed, bearded or rarely naked at the base, the interior erect often smaller or minute. *Stamens* three, inserted at the base of the outer segments of the perianth; *filaments* filiform or subulate: *anthers* oblong, affixed by the base. *Ovary* inferior, obsoletely three-cornered, three-celled; ovules numerous, horizontal, anatropous, in two rows in the central angle of the cells. *Style* triquetrous, the base often connate with the tube; *stigmas* three, petaloid-dilated, keeled above, channelled beneath, rarely two-lipped, opposite the stamens. *Capsule* coriaceous, trigonal or hexagonal, three-celled, loculicidally three-valved at the apex. *Seeds* numerous, plano-compressed, marginate.

———————

Iris setosa; not bearded; leaves subensiform somewhat shorter than the branched stem; spathes subacute scarious at the margin equalling the peduncles; tube of the perianth shorter than the ovary; the outer segments suborbicular with a broad claw, the inner very short wedge-shaped truncate cuspidate.

I. setosa, *Pallas, Bot. Reg.* 1847, t. 10.
I. brachycuspis, *Fischer MS.*}
I. cuspidata, *Fischer MS.* } *according to the Bot. Reg.*

———————

This very pretty plant has a somewhat creeping rhizome, and a roundish branched leafy stem somewhat taller than the leaves. The latter are sword-shaped. The spathes are as

254

long as the peduncles subacute with a scarious margin. The perianth is of a delicate lilac veined with red; its tube shorter than the ovary; the outer segments of its limb sub-orbicular with a broadish claw, the interior ones very short wedge-shaped truncate and cuspidate. The ovary is three-cornered, and is succeeded by a coriaceous oblong capsule.

This very pretty plant is said, by Dr. Fischer, to inhabit the northern part of Eastern Siberia, along the Lena, about Schigansk and Jakutzk, in Kamtchatka, Unalaschka, Escholtz's Bay, Chamisso's Island, &c. Its root is said to be poisonous, but we know not on what authority.

It was raised in the garden of the Horticultural Society of London from seeds received from Dr. Fischer, and flowered in May, 1846, for the first time.

It is a very hardy herbaceous species, growing from one to two feet in height, if planted in any good rich garden soil, and freely supplied with water during the growing season; but afterwards the plants should be kept rather dry, as they are very impatient of damp or wet during the winter months.

It is best increased by seeds treated in the usual way, but the young plants will not flower before the second year.

IRIS tridentata.

IRIS TRIDENTATA.

Three-toothed Flower de luce.

Nat. Ord. IRIDACEÆ.—IRIDS of Lindley.
Linnæan Class TRIANDRIA, Order MONOGYNIA.

IRIS, Linnæus.—Perianth corolline, superior ; tube short ; limb six-parted, the exterior segments most often reflexed, bearded or rarely naked at the base, the interior erect often smaller or minute. *Stamens* three, inserted at the base of the outer segments of the perianth ; *filaments* filiform or subulate ; *anthers* oblong, affixed by the base. *Ovary* inferior, obsoletely three-cornered, three-celled ; *ovules* numerous, horizontal, anatropous, in two rows in the central angle of the cells. *Style* triquetrous, the base often connate with the tube ; *stigmas* three, petaloid dilated, keeled above, channelled beneath, rarely two-lipped, opposite the stamens. *Capsule* coriaceous, trigonal or hexagonal, three-celled, loculicidally three-valved at the apex. *Seeds* numerous, plano-compressed, marginate.

I. tridentata ; not bearded ; leaves linear ensiform acuminate, stem about one-flowered longer than the leaves ; inner segments of the perianth very short unequally three-toothed, the central tooth acuminate.

I. tridentata, *Pursh Fl. Amer. Sept.* i. 30. *Sweet's Brit. Flow. Gard.,* t. 274.

I. tripelata, *Walt. Fl. Car.* 66.

The leaves of this species are ensiform, growing in a fan-shaped manner, from a foot to eighteen inches in length, tapering to the point, smooth, dark green, longitudinally striate, the margins smooth and transparent ; the stem-leaves are

255

shorter, curved inwards at the point, sheathing the stem at the base. The flower-stem is leafy, smooth, a little compressed, slightly angular, one or two-flowered, bearing a spathe of two bracts, which are two-flowered; the outer bract short, keeled, sharp-pointed the inner nearly three times the length, a little inflated, acute. The peduncle is smooth, slightly angular, about half the length of the outer bract. The perianth is tubular, six-parted, the tube a little inflated, smooth; the segments of the limb very unequal, outer ones broadly ovate, acute, not bearded, dark blue, veined with purple, the three inner ones very short and small, ligulate, veined, three-toothed at the point, the teeth short, the middle one being rather longer and acuminate. Stamens three, inserted in the tube; filaments smooth, rather succulent, a little flattened: anthers linear. Ovary smooth, below the flower, slightly triangular, a little swollen in the centre between the angles. Style smooth, triangular; stigmas three, sometimes increased to four, petal-form, of a blue purple, hollow underneath, and one-toothed on each side at the base, ribbed and furrowed on the upper side, through the centre, bifid at the point; the segments broadly lanceolate and tapering to a point.

Our drawing of this handsome and singular species was made in July, at the nursery of Messrs. Whitley and Co., at Fulham. The plant continued to produce flowers till the beginning of October. It is readily distinguished from all the other species, by the three inner segments of the perianth being very small, and three-toothed at the point. We have preferred the name of *tridentata*, as much more appropriate and expressive than that of *tripetala*, which has otherwise the right of superiority. It is a native of North America, and is rather a scarce plant.

It thrives well in the open border of the garden, and is pretty readily increased by dividing at the root.

The genus is named from *iris* the rainbow: from the various colours of the flowers in the genus.

256.

IRIS *nepalensis*.

IRIS NEPALENSIS.

Nepaul Flower de luce.

Nat. Ord. IRIDACEÆ—IRIDS of Lindley.
Linnæan Class TRIANDRIA, Order MONOGYNIA.

IRIS, Linnæus.—*Perianth* corolline, superior; tube short; limb six-parted, the exterior segments most often reflexed, bearded or rarely naked at the base, the interior erect often smaller or minute. *Stamens* three, inserted at the base of the outer segments of the perianth; *filaments* filiform or subulate; *anthers* oblong, affixed by the base. *Ovary* inferior, obsoletely three-cornered, three-celled; *ovules* numerous, horizontal, anatropous, in two rows in the central angle of the cells. *Style* triquetrous, the base often connate with the tube; *stigma* three, petaloid-dilated, keeled above, channelled beneath, rarely two-lipped, opposite the stamens. *Capsule* coriaceous, trigonal or hexagonal, three-celled, loculicidally three-valved at the apex. *Seeds* numerous, plano-compressed, marginate.

I. *nepalensis;* bearded; leaves linear ensiform plane nervose mucronate; tube of the perianth three times longer than the elongate obtusely three-cornered ovary, all the segments patent reflexed; stigmas fimbriate-erose.

I. nepalensis, *D. Don. Prod. Fl. Nep.* 54, not of *Bot. Reg. Sweet's Brit. Flow. Gard.* t. 5., t. 11.

The rhizome is fascicled and fleshy. The leaves are flatly distichous, linear ensiform, pale green, about eighteen inches in length, attenuated to a very sharp point, which terminates in a slender mucro sheathing each other at the base, strongly

256

nerved with several very prominent nerves, and other fainter ones. The flower-stem is produced from the root, solid, somewhat flexuose, cylindrical, producing from two to four short leaves, according to its strength, smooth and glossy; the stem leaves are inflated a little towards the base. The flowers are terminal, and axillary, larger than in *I. versicolor*, very handsome and delicate, of a pale blue colour, the outer segments striped with blue and pale yellow. The spathe is two-valved, producing two or three flowers in succession. The perianth is tubular, seated on a bluntly three-sided ovary; its tube very long and slender rather longer than the spathe; its limb six-parted, the segments spreading, all more or less reflexed, and slightly notched at the points, the three outer ones rather broadest, oblong ovate, attenuated towards the base, the ground of a straw-colour, elegantly striped with blue, pale straw-colour at the back; on the upper side is a handsome crest from the base to above half way up, fringed with yellow; the three inner segments are oblong, attenuated towards the base, a little undulate or curled at the margins, of a delicate pale blue, faintly veined. Stamens three, inserted at the base of the outer segments, at the summit of the tube: filaments smooth, white: anthers linear. The ovary is bluntly three-sided, smooth and glossy; the style short, smooth; the stigmas three, petal-like, attenuated to the base, broad at the end, deeply cleft, keeled on the upper side and concave below, jagged at the edges, and more so at the points, which are erosely fimbriate.

Our drawing of this beautiful *Iris* was taken at the latter end of June, at the nursery of Messrs. Whitley and Co., at Fulham, where it was raised from seed received from Nepal. It differs from all the species with which we are acquainted, by its fleshy roots, resembling those of a *Hemerocallis*. The *I. nepalénsis* of the Botanical Register is a European plant probably identical with *I. pallida*.

The present species thrives well in a peat bed, but we would advise its being covered a little in severe frosty weather. It may be increased by dividing at the root.

IRIS *lutea*.

IRIS AUREA.

Golden Flower de luce.

Nat. Ord. IRIDACEÆ.—IRIDS of Lindley.
Linnæan Class TRIANDRIA, Order MONOGYNIA.

IRIS, Linnæus.—*Perianth* corolline, superior ; tube short ; limb six-parted, the exterior segments most often reflexed, bearded or rarely naked at the base, the interior erect often smaller or minute. *Stamens* three, inserted at the base of the outer segments of the perianth ; *filaments* filiform or subulate ; *anthers* oblong, affixed by the base. *Ovary* inferior, obsoletely three-cornered, three-celled ; *ovules* numerous, horizontal, anatropous, in two rows in the central angle of the cells. *Style* triquetrous, the base often connate with the tube ; *stigmas* three, petaloid-dilated, keeled above, channelled beneath, rarely two-lipped, opposite the stamens. *Capsule* coriaceous, trigonal or hexagonal, three-celled, loculicidally three-valved at the apex. *Seeds* numerous, plano-compressed, marginate.

I. aurea ; not bearded ; leaves ensiform about equalling the many-flowered scape ; outer segments of the perianth ovate undulate narrowing into a claw equalling the acute bifid stigmas ; inner segments undulate acute.
I. aurea, *Lindley in Bot. Reg.* 1847, t. 59.

A showy perennial herbaceous plant with the sword-shaped leaves common among Irises. These leaves are as tall as the many-flowered scape, which is furnished with acute imbricate leafy scales longer than the tube of the perianth. The flowers are deep yellow, the exterior segments of the perianth ovate undulate narrowed into a claw which about equals the acute bifid stigmas; the inner segments are undulated and acute.

This Iris was raised by Messrs. Whitley and Osborne of Fulham, from Indian seeds presented to them by Dr. Royle. The specimen here figured was communicated to Dr. Lindley in July, 1846, with the following note:—"It flowers very freely, with the habit of *Iris ochroleuca*, and grows as tall." Possibly it is merely an Indian form of that species; but if it be so, it presents points of distinction which render it at least a well marked variety. It differs from *I. ochroleuca* in the sepals and petals being more lanceolate and wavy at the edge, and in its bright golden yellow colour. In the former respect it is more like *I. halophila* (Bot. Mag. t. 1131), but the flowers are much larger, and the base of the sepals not more than half as wide.

We do not find any notice of such a plant in the works of Indian Botanists.

It will be an acceptable addition to the list of showy hardy perennials, growing in good garden soil, and increased by divisions.

IRIS hamatophylla.

IRIS HÆMATOPHYLLA.

Red-leaved Flower de luce.

————

Nat. Ord. IRIDACEÆ—IRIDS of Lindley.
Linnæan Class TRIANDRIA, Order MONOGYNIA.

————

IRIS, Linnæus.—*Perianth* corolline, superior; tube short; limb six-parted, the exterior segments most often reflexed, bearded or rarely naked at the base, the interior erect often smaller or minute. *Stamens* three, inserted at the base of the outer segments of the perianth; *filaments* filiform or subulate; *anthers* oblong, affixed by the base. *Ovary* inferior, obsoletely three-cornered, three-celled; *ovules* numerous, horizontal, anatropous, in two rows in the central angle of the cells. *Style* triquetrous, the base often connate with the tube; *stigmas* three, petaloid-dilated, keeled above, channelled beneath, rarely two-lipped, opposite the stamens. *Capsule* coriaceous, trigonal or hexagonal, three-celled, loculicidally three-valved at the apex. *Seeds* numerous, plano-compressed, marginate.

————

I. hæmatophylla; not bearded; leaves linear, lax, much longer than the scape; spathes two opposite acute; flowers pedicellate; germen three-cornered.

I. hæmatophylla, *Fischer MS. Sweet in Brit. Flow. Gard.* t. 118.

I. sanguinea, *Rœmer et Schultes.*

I. Nertschinskia, *Loddiges, Bot. Cab.* t. 1843.

I. sibirica, var. *of authors.*

————

This plant is a tufted perennial, having leaves longer than the scape, weak, linear acute, slightly twisted, striate, and when young more or less of a blood red or purple colour, becoming at length pale yellowish green, and purple at the

258

base only. The scape is long, striate, a little flattened, two or three-flowered, and furnished with two opposite acute keeled sheaths, enclosing the base of the peduncles, which latter are obsoletely three-sided. The perianth is six-parted, its tube very short, or scarcely present; the outer segments of its limb largest, reflexed, obovate narrowed at the base, in some flowers pale blue variegated with purple and yellow network from about the middle, in others darker blue also variegated with white yellow and purple; the inner segments are erect at first, incurved narrower acute, rather darker and slightly variegated at the base. The three stamens are inserted in the base of the segments. The style is short; the stigmas three, petal-like, purple, bifid at the point and a little jagged at the sides.

This handsome species is generally known in collections by the name of *Iris sanguinea*, a name tending to mislead, as implying rather red flowers than red leaves. Dr. Fischer therefore, substituted instead, the much more appropriate name *hæmatophylla*. This plant, with several others, has been united with *I. sibirica*, but we consider it decidedly distinct; its time of flowering is fully a month earlier than that species, and in cold springs, the flowers are often much injured, if not entirely destroyed, the flowers showing themselves before the leaves are grown of sufficient length to render them any protection.

Our figure was made from a plant which bloomed at the beginning of April, in the nursery of the late Mr. Colvill. It is a native of Siberia. The leaves, when young, have always a red tinge; in some plants they are quite red or purple, but the colour both of the leaves and flowers varies considerably on different plants.

It grows very freely in the common garden soil, in a dry situation, and may be increased by seeds, or by dividing at the root. We would advise its being planted in an elevated and exposed situation to keep it from growing as late as possible in spring, as by that means its flowers would be more likely to escape injury from frost.

259

IRIS *fœtidissima* G. *Reeve*

IRIS FRAGRANS.

Sweet-scented Flower de luce.

Nat. Ord. IRIDACEÆ.—IRIDS of Lindley.
Linnæan Class TRIANDRIA, Order MONOGYNIA.

IRIS, Linnæus.—Perianth corolline, superior; tube short; limb six-parted, the exterior segments most often reflexed, bearded or rarely naked at the base, the interior erect often smaller or minute. *Stamens* three, inserted at the base of the outer segments of the perianth; *filaments* filiform or subulate; *anthers* oblong, affixed by the base. *Ovary* inferior, obsoletely three-cornered, three-celled; *ovules* numerous, horizontal, anatropous, in two rows in the central angle of the cells. *Style* triquetrous, the base often connate with the tube; *stigmas* three, petaloid-dilated, keeled above, channelled beneath, rarely two-lipped, opposite the stamens. *Capsule* coriaceous, trigonal or hexagonal, three-celled, loculicidally three-valved at the apex. *Seeds* numerous, plano-compressed, marginate.

I. fragrans; not bearded; leaves narrow ensiform glaucescent, as long as the many-flowered stem; ovary fusiform longer than the herbaceous bracts; perianth tube none, limb of the sepals rhomboid entire, of the petals spathulate-lanceolate very entire narrow at the base as long as the sepals; styles cleft.

I. fragrans, *Lindley in Bot. Reg. 1840, t. 1.*

A fine showy hardy perennial, with long narrow erect leaves, and a tallish branched flower-stem bearing several blossoms. The flowers are rather small in size the parts being much narrowed; the tube is not developed; the outer

259

segments of the limb have a narrow stalk-like base, and a broader rhomboidal recurved blade; they are blue variegated with white; the inner segments are narrower and erect of a blueish-lilac.

This very distinct species of Iris is a native of the North of India, where it was found by Professor Royle. " In habit," writes Dr. Lindley, " it resembles the *I. decora* of Wallich, which is the *I. nepalensis* of Don, but its flowers are altogether different; it is also extremely like the *I. sulcata* of Wallich's Indian herbarium, no. 5049, referred to *I. decora* by Professor Royle, but from which it appears to be distinguished by the form of the fruit, which, in *I. fragrans*, when young, is fusiform and longer than the bracts, while in *I. sulcata* it is oblong, and shorter than the bracts. *I. longifolia*, a Cashmere species, figured in the *Illustrations of the Botany of the Himalayan Mountains*, resembles this in the form of the leaves, but they are described as being scabrous at the margin; moreover the scape is very short and one-flowered in that plant, and the lobes of the style are said to be entire; in the absence of a tube to the flower the two correspond."

The accompanying figure was taken in the garden of the Horticultural Society, from plants raised in 1835, from seeds presented by Dr. Royle.

The fragrance of the flowers of this species, in addition to its pretty appearance, makes it a desirable border plant. It is found to be a very hardy perennial, requiring about the same treatment as the common *Iris sibirica*, growing freely in any rich soil, and blossoming about the end of June. It may be easily increased by dividing the old root-stock.

IRIS *Doriana.*

IRIS DONIANA.

Don's Flower de luce.

Nat. Ord. IRIDACEÆ.—IRIDS of Lindley.
Linnæan Class TRIANDRIA, Order MONOGYNIA.

IRIS, Linnæus.—*Perianth* corolline, superior; tube short; limb six-parted, the exterior segments most often reflexed, bearded or rarely naked at the base, the interior erect often smaller or minute. *Stamens* three, inserted at the base of the outer segments of the perianth; *filaments* filiform or subulate; *anthers* oblong, affixed by the base. *Ovary* inferior, obsoletely three-cornered, three-celled; *ovules* numerous, horizontal, anatropous, in two rows in the central angle of the cells. *Style* triquetrous, the base often connate with the tube; *stigmas* three, petaloid-dilated, keeled above, channelled beneath, rarely two-lipped, opposite the stamens. *Capsule* coriaceous, trigonal or hexagonal, three-celled, loculicidally three-valved at the apex. *Seeds* numerous, plano-compressed, marginate.

I. Doniana; not bearded; spathe equalling or longer than the flowers; outer segments spathulate-oblong retuse, about twice as broad as the lanceolate-oblong acute inner ones; stigmas about twice as long as the perianth.

I. Doniana, *Spach. Hist. Pl. Phan.* xiii. 34. *Walp. Annales* i. 821.
I. biglumis, *D. Don in Sweet's Brit. Flow. Gard.* 2. s.. t. 187.

This species has a creeping rhizome. The scape is round, about three inches high, entirely enclosed by a pair of leaves, from the bosom of which it issues. The leaves are narrow ensiform acuminate, erect, of a dull glaucous green, dark red

260

at the base, exceeding the scape, and lengthening considerably after the flowering season. The spathe is composed of two broad ovate-oblong acute, membranous, nearly equal leaves of which the edges are scariose, and over-lapping towards the base. The flowers are usually two in number, sessile, pale blue; the segments about equal in size and form, narrow, rather spathulate than lanceolate, the outer three reflexed, rather broader and paler than the inner ones, which are erect, but hardly connivent; the disk is of a whitish colour, marked with numerous purple veins and spots. The stigmas are linear, cloven, deeply and sharply serrated, of a deeper shade of blue.

This pretty Iris is very nearly related to *I. spuria*, but apparently distinct from all the varieties of that species by its shorter stem, the broader and glumaceous bracts, and the nearly equal segments of its flowers. It is a native of Siberia.

The species was introduced by Mr. Anderson, from seed communicated by Dr. Fischer to the Botanic Garden, Chelsea, where our drawing was taken in the early part of the summer months.

Like the other herbaceous Irises, this species is found to succeed when cultivated in ordinary light garden soil; and is increased by division of the root.

IRIS *verna*.

IRIS VERNA.

Vernal American Flower de luce.

Nat. Ord. IRIDACEÆ.—IRIDS of Lindley.
Linnæan Class TRIANDRIA, Order MONOGYNIA.

IRIS, Linnæus.—*Perianth* corolline, superior; tube short; limb six-parted, the exterior segments most often reflexed, bearded or rarely naked at the base, the interior erect often smaller or minute. *Stamens* three, inserted at the base of the outer segments of the perianth; *filaments* filiform or subulate; *anthers* oblong, affixed by the base. *Ovary* inferior, obsoletely three-cornered, three-celled; *ovules* numerous, horizontal, anatropous, in two rows in the central angle of the cells. *Style* triquetrous, the base often connate with the tube; *stigmas* three, petaloid-dilated, keeled above, channelled beneath, rarely two-lipped, opposite the stamens. *Capsule* coriaceous, trigonal or hexagonal, three-celled, loculicidally three-valved at the apex. *Seeds* numerous, plano-compressed, marginate.

I. verna; not bearded, stemless, one-flowered; leaves linear-ensiform rigid acute glaucescent; segments of the perianth subequal; capsules obsoletely three-cornered.

I. verna. *Michaux Fl. Amer.* i. 22. *Sweet's Brit. Fl. Gard.* t. 68.

In this very pretty Iris the rhizomes are slender creeping and of a reddish colour. The leaves are radical, linear-ensiform, rigidly coriaceous, acute, slightly glaucous, tinged with red at the base, about a foot in length. The scape is one-flowered, sessile, or nearly so, sheathed at the base with short leaf-like bracts. The tube of the perianth is slightly but bluntly triangular, about two inches long; the segments are jointed on the tube, the inner and outer divisions nearly equal, with long slender claws, oblong-ovate, of a beautiful bright blue; the three exterior segments marked with an oblong orange-yellow stripe, edged and spotted with black, and having a central slightly raised, scarcely villous line; the inner ones of one colour, at first connivent, afterwards spreading flat like the outer ones. There are three stamens inserted in the base of the segments at the summit of the tube. The style is short; the stigmas three, petal-like, linear-oblong, deeply bifid and toothed at the edges, keeled inwards.

The late Mr. Colvill received plants of the present species many years since from North America, which is its native country. It flowers about May.

This is certainly one of the most beautiful of all the dwarf species of Iris, and appears to grow as freely as any of them, when planted in a rich light soil, flowering the beginning of May. Its flowers possess a considerable degree of fragrance. The plants may be increased by dividing at the root.

IRIS *dichotoma*

IRIS DICHOTOMA.

Forked-petaled Flower de luce.

Nat. Ord. IRIDACEÆ.—IRIDS of Lindley.
Linnæan Class TRIANDRIA, Order MONOGYNIA.

IRIS Linnæus.—Perianth corolline, superior; tube short; limb six-parted, the exterior segments most often reflexed, bearded or rarely naked at the base, the interior erect often smaller or minute. *Stamens* three, inserted at the base of the outer segments of the perianth; *filaments* filiform or subulate; *anthers* oblong, affixed by the base. *Ovary* inferior, obsoletely three-cornered, three-celled; *ovules* numerous, horizontal, anatropous, in two rows in the central angle of the cells. *Style* triquetrous, the base often connate with the tube; *stigmas* three, petaloid-dilated, keeled above, channelled beneath, rarely two-lipped, opposite the stamens. *Capsule* coriaceous, trigonal or hexagonal, three-celled, loculicidally three-valved at the apex. *Seeds* numerous, plano-compressed, marginate.

I. dichotoma; leaves falcately sword-shaped; scapes terete, paniculately-branched; spathes terminal, two-leaved, many-flowered; tube of the perianth wanting, the outer segments of the limb partially bearded, the inner bifid at the apex.

I. dichotoma, *Willdenow Sp. Pl.* i. 230. *Sweet in Brit. Fl. Gard.* t. 96.

I. pomeridiana, *Fischer MS.* fide *Sweet.*

From the rhizome, rises the stem a foot to eighteen inches in height. The leaves are ensiform, more or less falcate, of a glaucous green colour. The scape is cylindrical, paniculately branching, leafy, smooth; the sheaths terminal, many-

262

flowered, two-leaved, the leaflets ovate concave with scariose points. The peduncles are long and slender, about twice the length of the sheaths. The perianth is divided nearly to the base into six segments; of these the outer ones are linear-oblong obtuse with crenulate points, reflexed from about the middle, of a light purple tinged with brown, and variegated near the base, and slightly bearded with a large white patch and more or less spotted with purple in the centre; the inner segments are obovate attenuated to the base, the points bifid or forked and sometimes toothed, of a light purple. Stamens three, inserted in the base of the segments, about half the length of the stigmas. Style short; stigmas three, petal-like, channelled at the back, and keeled inwards, deeply bifid, the segments taper-pointed and twisted.

This beautiful and very distinct species of *Iris*, in habit approaches the genus *Pardanthus*, and appears to be the connecting link between the two genera. It also differs from all the other known species, in the time of expansion of its flowers, which never open till the afternoon, which circumstance induced Dr. Fischer to give it the appropriate name of *I. pomeridiana*. It is a native of Dahuria. Our drawing was taken at the Chelsea Botanic Garden, in the summer of 1824. It had been raised from seed received from Dr. Fischer.

The species is rather tender, suffering much from a superabundance of moisture, so that it should be planted in a dry open situation, and in a light soil, where the wet will pass off readily. It is also well to preserve some plants of it in pots, to be placed in frames in very wet or very cold weather. These can be planted in the borders in spring. It may be increased by seeds, or by dividing at the root.

263

IRIS *caucasica*

IRIS CAUCASICA.

Caucasian Flower de luce.

Nat. Ord. IRIDACEÆ.—IRIDS of Lindley.
Linnæan Class TRIANDRIA, Order MONOGYNIA.

IRIS, Linnæus.—*Perianth* corolline, superior; tube short; limb six-parted, the exterior segments most often reflexed, bearded or rarely naked at the base, the interior erect often smaller or minute. *Stamens* three, inserted at the base of the outer segments of the perianth; *filaments* filiform or subulate; *anthers* oblong, affixed by the base. *Ovary* inferior, obsoletely three-cornered, three-celled; *ovules* numerous, horizontal, anatropous, in two rows in the central angle of the cells. *Style* triquetrous, the base often connate with the tube; *stigmas* three, petaloid-dilated, keeled above, channelled beneath, rarely two-lipped, opposite the stamens. *Capsule* coriaceous, trigonal or hexagonal, three-celled, loculicidally three-valved at the apex. *Seeds* numerous, plano-compressed, marginate.

I. caucasica; not bearded; leaves falcate conduplicate longer than the usually two-flowered scape; outer segments of the perianth bearing a rugged crest, the inner minute lanceolate reflexed; stigmas very obtuse retuse.

I. caucasica, *Steven Dec. Pl. Iber,* ex *Bieberstein Fl. Taur. Cauc.* i. 33. *Sweet in Brit. Flower Garden,* t. 255.

The bulb of this species is tunicate, of the size and form of that of *I. persica,* clothed with thin membranaceous scales, and producing from the base several large fleshy roots. The leaves are channelled, distichous or fan-shaped, lanceolate

263

falcate conduplicate taper-pointed, glaucous on the outside green within, longitudinally striated with white lines, and margined with white. The scape is shorter than the leaves, generally two-flowered; the spathe inflated, striate. The flowers are straw-coloured; the tube of the perianth slender; the outer segments of the limb ovate obtuse, marked with a rugged yellow crest, but not bearded; the inner segments small lanceolate acute, undulate, slender at the base, reflexed or bent downwards. Stamens three. Ovary nearly cylindrical. Stigmas three, large, erect, about the size of the largest segments, very broad at the end, transparent, bluntly rounded and retuse.

This very rare plant was flowered by the late Hon. and Rev. W. Herbert, of Spofforth, Yorkshire, in February, 1828, in a pot plunged in a dry border, sloping to the south, without any protection, in which situation it had been kept six or seven years, since it had been first raised from seed. It is a native of Mount Caucasus, and is mentioned by Marschall Bieberstein as being frequent on sunny hills round Tiflis, flowering early in spring. The bulb nearly resembles the Persian Iris, as does the habit of the plant. *I. alata* is also a nearly related species.

The present species will probably hardly become common in our collections, except seeds or bulbs of it are introduced abundantly from its native mountains. It also requires more than ordinary care to preserve it in good health, it being very liable to rot, if in too moist a situation. A dry border of light sandy soil, where the wet passes off readily, is the most congenial situation for it.

264

264

IRIS *reticulata.*

IRIS RETICULATA.

Netted Flower de luce.

Nat. Ord. IRIDACEÆ.—IRIDS of Lindley.
Linnæan Class TRIANDRIA, Order MONOGYNIA.

IRIS, Linnæus.—Perianth corolline, superior; tube short; limb six-parted, the exterior segments most often reflexed, bearded or rarely naked at the base, the interior erect often smaller or minute. *Stamens* three, inserted at the base of the outer segments of the perianth: *filaments* filiform or subulate; *anthers* oblong, affixed by the base. *Ovary* inferior, obsoletely three-cornered, three-celled; *ovules* numerous, horizontal, anatropous, in two rows in the central angle of the cells. *Style* triquetrous, the base often connate with the tube; *stigmas* three, petaloid-dilated, keeled above, channelled beneath, rarely two-lipped, opposite the stamens. *Capsule* coriaceous, trigonal or hexagonal, three-celled, loculicidally three-valved at the apex. *Seeds* numerous, plano-compressed, marginate.

I. reticulata; bulbous; leaves tetragonal; not bearded; inner segments of the limb of the perianth lanceolate-spathulate erect elongated: stigmas obtuse two-lobed.

    I. reticulata. *Bieberstein Fl. Taur. Cauc.* i. 34. *D. Don in Sweet's Brit. Flow. Gard.* 2. s., t. 189.

    This plant produces an ovate bulb covered with several reticulated brown coats. The leaves, issuing from a double spathaceous keeled unequal sheath, are long slender hollow tetragonal glaucous, copiously furnished with minute white dots, terminated by a white point, from a span to a foot or

264

more in length ; the sides concave, smooth, with a conspicuous nerve, and blunt angles. The flowers are solitary, purple ; the peduncle scarcely an inch long, three-sided ; the spathe composed of two unequal linear mucronate keeled cartilaginous nerved valves, the inner one smaller. The perianth tube is slender, obtusely three-sided, about an inch and a half long, greenish white, and furrowed, the angles marked with a blue line ; the outer segments of the limb are oblong rather cuneiform, spreading, concave, with a stout greenish midrib, the ground of a pale purple, marked with deeper coloured veins, the apex recurved, and slightly mucronulate, of a deep violet, rather inclining to blue towards the centre, where is an oblong orange spot, marked with violet dots ; the three inner ones are erect, longer, lanceolate or somewhat spathulate, bluntish, slightly waved, narrowed towards the base, uniformly purple. The ovary has three blunt angles, each furnished with an elevated ridge. The stigmas are oblong, about as long and rather broader than the outer segments of the perianth, and of the same uniform purple colour as the inner segments ; the upper lip formed of two rounded, finely serrated, recurved lobes, the lower very short, and almost obsolete.

We are indebted to Messrs. Whitley and Co. (now Osborn) of the Fulham Nursery, for the opportunity of figuring this rare and beautiful Iris, which had been received by them from M. Hartwiss, Director of the Imperial Gardens, at Nikita, in the Crimea. It appears to have been first introduced to our gardens in 1821, but the plant was afterwards lost. It blossoms early in March.

This remarkable species agrees with *I. tuberosa* in its leaves, but the flower is very different, more resembling that of the normal group of the genus ; and we know of no species with which it can well be compared ; though it must be placed near to *I. Xiphium*, and *I. Xiphioides*, to which it approaches in habit, and in its bulbiform roots. The species was originally discovered in Georgia.

The plant requires a light rich soil, and the shelter of a pit or frame in winter. It is increased by offsets, and by seeds, which become perfect if the season is favourable, and care is taken to protect the plant from the wet, and to admit a free circulation of air when it is in flower.

I. Lomath del   IRIS *longifolia*   *W.J.H.*

IRIS LONGIFOLIUS.

Long-leaved Flower de luce.

Nat. Ord. IRIDACEÆ.—IRIDS of Lindley.
Linnæan Class TRIANDRIA, Order MONOGYNIA.

IRIS, Linnæus.—Perianth corolline, superior; tube short; limb six-parted, the exterior segments most often reflexed, bearded or rarely naked at the base, the interior erect often smaller or minute. *Stamens* three, inserted at the base of the outer segments of the perianth; *filaments* filiform or subulate; *anthers* oblong, affixed by the base. *Ovary* inferior, obsoletely three-cornered, three-celled; *ovules* numerous, horizontal, anatropous, in two rows in the central angle of the cells. *Style* triquetrous, the base often connate with the tube; *stigmas* three, petaloid-dilated, keeled above, channelled beneath, rarely two-lipped, opposite the stamens. *Capsule* coriaceous, trigonal or hexagonal, three-celled, loculicidally three-valved at the apex. *Seeds* numerous, plano-compressed, marginate.

I. longifolius; radical leaves very long thick regularly quadrangular striated glaucous, those of the stem short somewhat inflated at the base, acute at the apex; scape one-flowered; outer segments of perianth obovate emarginate reflexed, the inner cucullate at the base, attenuate and acute at the apex, lacerato-serrate.
I. longifolius, *Spach Ann. Scien. Nat.* 3. s., v. 91.
Hermodactylus longifolius, *Sweet in Brit. Flower Gard.* 2. s., t. 146.

This very curious plant produces root tubers which vary from one to two in number. The leaves are tightly surrounded at the base by white soft somewhat membranaceous sheaths, and are themselves very glaucescent, almost white, quadrangular, longitudinally striated; those produced from the base frequently three to four feet in length, the largest above half an inch in circumference; the angles are sharp edged; those of the scape are rather inflated towards the base, tapering upwards, and rising only to the base of the flower. The flower stem grows about nine inches high, and is smooth and rounded. The spathe is leaf-like, persistent, rigid, one-valved, extending to the top of the flower when expanded, somewhat ventricose over the ovary, but tapering upwards to a sharp point. The perianth has a short tube, and is deeply six-parted; the three large outer segments about three inches in length, narrowing to the base, curved a little inwards from the sides, green slightly tinged with purple nearly to the bend, a pale yellow line extending down the centre to the base; at the bend they are considerably curved backwards, and have two greenish white marks edged with dark purple; from thence to the point they are broadly obovate-ovate with a slight notch at the point bright velvety purplish brown on the upper side, edged with green, green at the back and hollow in the recurved part; the three small inner segments are very small, curved inwards from the base a considerable way up, thus cucullate, or hollow, and then becoming abruptly narrow, and terminating in a very slender point. The three stamens are inserted in the base of the perianth, and pressed close to the back of the stigma, with flat filaments inserted in the base of the anthers, which are linear and discharge yellow pollen. The ovary is oblong, six-lined, tapering to the flower, considerably below it; the style short; the stigmas three, deeply two-cleft, keeled on the inside, and hollow at the back, lacerately-sawed at the margin, the segments spreading right and left, sharp pointed. The capsule is oblong-elliptical, tapering considerably towards the base, and a little towards the point.

The drawing of this singular *Iris* was made from a plant brought from Naples, and which first flowered with Mr. Sweet in June, 1832. Sweet distinguished three species which had been confused under the name of *I. tuberosa* from the circumstance of the short description "foliis tetragonis" being applicable to them all. They are besides the present one, *I. tuberosa* and *I. bispathaceus*.

These somewhat tender plants may be successfully grown on a south border, protected by a mat in winter. They should be planted in a good sandy loam, and are increased by careful division.

VIESSEUXIA *glaucopis*

VIESSEUXIA GLAUCOPIS.

Ocellate Viesseuxia.

Nat. Ord. IRIDACEÆ.—IRIDS of Lindley.
Linnæan Class TRIANDRIA, Order MONOGYNIA.

VIESSEUXIA, Roche.—*Perianth* corolline superior, rotately hexaphyllous, the exterior segments narrowly unguiculate at the base, often bearded, the interior many times smaller, subulate or tricuspidate. *Stamens* three, placed on the epigynous disk, the filaments connate into a tube, the anthers oblong affixed by the base. *Ovary* inferior oblong-prismatical, three-celled; *ovules* numerous horizontal anatropous, in two rows in the central angle of the cells; *style* short filiform; *stigmas* three, petaloid dilated, two lobed, opposite the stamens. *Capsule* coriaceous, obtusely three-cornered, three-celled, loculicidally three-valved. *Seeds* numerous.

V. glaucopis; perianth bearded, the interior segments trifid; lobes of the stigmas unequally-oblong repand-crenate; leaves glabrous.
V. glaucopis, *DeCandolle Ann. Mus.* ii. 141.
Iris pavonia, *Curtis Bot. Mag.* t. 168; not of others.

This beautiful plant has bulbiform tubers about the size of a filbert. The stem is about a foot high, slender round flexuose solid glabrous geniculate, slightly striated, grass-green. The radical leaves are about twice the length of the stem, narrow linear flat, ribbed and furrowed, of a glaucous green attenuated at both ends; those of the stem are about three in number, the two upper ones but partially developed, the lowest one longer than the stem, channelled, convolute at the base, ribbed beneath. The sheaths are entire, the upper ones terminating in a bristle-shaped point. The spathes are two-valved, convolute, slightly ventricose, with a scariose

266

border, finely striated, bristle-pointed, the lower one shorter. The perianth is deeply parted into six segments, the three outer ones broadly cuneate, entire, and even at the edge, of a pure white, streaked with purple especially beneath, furnished just above the claw with a broad round azure spot which has an irregularly lobed violet border, the claws cuneate lined with purple spots and copiously bearded with yellow hairs; the three inner ones are scarcely half the length, cuneate, convolute, erect, of an olive colour towards the base, white above, and spotted with violet, three-lobed at the top, the lateral lobes broad and rounded with entire wavy margins, the intermediate one longer, linear pointed, reflexed. The three white filaments are united into a cylindrical column; the anthers adpressed to the back of the stigmas, linear, mucronate, with two adnate parallel cells, which are free and slightly divaricate at the base. The ovary is bluntly three-sided, half an inch long, three-celled, with three rows of ovules in each cell; stigmas three, petal-like, ligulate, bilabiate, cloven, with oblong semilunar connivent lobes, irregularly repand and crenate at the outer edge, white and veiny, pale blue, and glabrous at the base, the outer lip very short, truncate, with two teeth.

This very elegant plant is not surpassed in beauty by any of its congeners. Don considered it a variety of *V. tricuspis*, perceiving no difference, except colour, whereby to distinguish it; and he considered that colour, which in many exogenous families, is almost a certain indication of specific distinction, is a very fallacious character among the *Irideæ* and other *Monocotyledons*. It is a native of the Cape. The accompanying drawing was taken at the late Mr. Colvill's nursery, in May.

The Cape *Irideæ* do not necessarily require a greenhouse for their successful cultivation. All that they require is protection from frost, and this can be best afforded them in a frame, which may be removed entirely in fine weather. A warm sunny border should be selected for their culture, and the earth removed to the depth of a foot or eighteen inches, and replaced by a mixture of light loam vegetable mould and river sand. The bulbs should be taken up in the autumn, and replanted about the middle of January, the larger ones being carefully selected from the rest. The earth will require to be renewed every two or three years.

267

MORÆA Tenoreana

MORÆA TENOREANA.

Tenore's Moræa.

Nat. Ord. IRIDACEÆ.—IRIDS of Lindley.
Linnæan Class TRIANDRIA, Order MONOGYNIA.

MORÆA, Linnæus.—Perianth corolline superior; tube very short; limb six-parted spreading, the interior segments smaller, convolute after flowering. *Stamens* three, inserted in the tube of the perianth; *filaments* distinct; *anthers* oblong, affixed by their base. *Ovary* inferior oblong prismatical; *ovules* numerous horizontal anatropous, in two rows in the central angles of the cells; *style* slender triquetrous; *stigmas* three petaloid-dilated bi-tri-fid, opposite the stamens. *Capsule* membranaceous, bluntly three-cornered, three-celled. *Seeds* numerous angulate.

M. Tenoreana; radical leaves two, very long, involute, exteriorly striate; scape knee-jointed, somewhat branched, many-flowered; perianth six-parted, the segments emarginate with a point, the exterior tuberculately bearded at the base.

M. Tenoreana, *Sweet in British Flower Garden*, t. 110.
Iris fugax, *Tenore Fl. Neapol.* i. 15, t. 4.

The bulb-tuber of this pretty species is about the size of a large nut, and clothed with a coarse light brown reticulated cartilagineo-fibrous shell. The leaves, two growing from the root, are from a foot to fifteen inches in length, tapering to a fine point, bifariously spreading, smooth and glossy, the sides folded in, so as to leave a large channel in the centre, the

267

outside striped with numerous small longitudinal lines. The scape pointed, more or less branched, from a foot to fifteen inches high; from each joint grows a sheath which is about three inches long, striped with numerous dark green lines, the lower part tubular, clasping the stem, the upper part membranaceous, and tapering to a point. The perianth has a long slender nearly cylindrical tube, of a greenish white, irregularly marked with a few red streaks; this is divided above into six petal-like segments, of a bright blue colour; the outer segments unguiculate, from about the middle ovate, reflexed a little, the points broadly emarginate, with a small mucro in the middle from the bend to the base tuberculately bearded in a longitudinal yellow line, and spotted with purple on each side, terminated above the bend in a large white patch, from which a purple line runs to the point; the inner segments are scarcely half the size of the outer ones, also emarginate with a mucro at the point. Stamens three; filaments *smooth;* anthers linear; sharp pointed; pollen white. Style slender, smooth, terminated by three forked petal-like stigmas.

Our drawing of this interesting species was taken at the nursery of the late Mr. Colvill. It is a native of Naples. The species is nearly related to *Morœa Sisyrinchium*, but differs sufficiently in the shape of its petals, and its membranaceous not leafy sheaths. It continues flowering in succession for a considerable time.

It requires to be planted in a dry warm border of light sandy soil; or if planted in a pot, in an equal mixture of light turfy loam, peat, and sand, and protected in a frame in winter, it will succeed very well.

FERRARIA *obtusifolia.*

FERRARIA OBTUSIFOLIA.

Blunt-leaved Ferraria.

Nat. Ord. IRIDACEÆ.—IRIDS of Lindley.
Linnæan Class MONADELPHIA, Order TRIANDRIA.

FERRARIA, Linnæus.—*Perianth* six parted petaloid, the segments undulato-crisped, the inner ones smaller. *Stamens* three, the filaments coalescing into a tube spreading at the apex, anthers two-lobed. *Stigmas* three, pencilliform. *Capsule* three-celled, inferior.

F. obtusifolia; stem erect branched many-flowered; leaves distichous ensiform, obtuse, glaucous, keeled on both sides, lobes of the anthers approximate.

F. obtusifolia, *Sweet in British Flower Garden,* t. 148.

The corm or rootstock tuberous, smooth, not unlike a potato. The stem is erect, smooth but glaucous, cylindrical, about eighteen inches in height, very much branched; the branches again branching and crowded. The leaves are distichous, sheathing the stem at the base, ensiform, obtuse, but terminated with a small point in the middle, sharply keeled from the base to the point on both sides, and covered with a glaucous gloss, which easily rubs off; the leaves on the middle of the stem are longest, as long as the stem, the upper ones becoming gradually shorter. The flowers are numerous; the spathes crowded, two-valved, ventricose, scarcely acute, striate with numerous small lines, the margins membrana-

268

ceous; the upper one double the length of the other; another membranaceous spathe encloses the flower before expansion. The perianth is deeply divided into six petal-like segments, the three outer ones being nearly double the size of the others, reflexed from about the middle, the bases forming a sort of bowl, below the bend striped with white and purple, above the bend about half way to the point of a rich velvety brown colour, in the middle of which on the smaller segments is a small white spot, the edges and points elegantly curled, of a yellowish brown colour. Stamens three; filaments spotted, joined in a tube at the base, the points spreading; anthers large, two-lobed, the lobes open at the base, but approaching each other; pollen orange-coloured. Ovary smooth, acutely three-sided; style smooth, about the length of the stamens; stigmas three, each bifid, and divided into numerous bristle-like segments like a pencil, brown at the base the points yellow.

This beautiful and distinct species was introduced from the Cape by Mr. Synnot, and flowered in the collection of Mr. Colvill, where our drawing was made. It flowers in autumn, producing a large number of flowers, which, continue to open in succession, for nearly two months.

As the bulb, or rather tuber is large, and not unlike a potato, it will require to be planted deep in the ground—fully six inches. It should be planted out the end of March, or beginning of April, in a bed composed of a light sandy soil, such as is used for tulips, or other choice bulbous roots. After flowering, and when the stems are beginning to decay, the root should be taken up and laid to dry, out of the reach of frost, till the following spring; it would not be safe to let it remain in the ground all the winter, except it was well covered, and in a warm sheltered situation.

Ferraria is named in honour of J. B. Ferrari an Italian botanist.

269

L.D.Smith Del.

MUSCARI *macrocarpum.*

Halderia

MUSCARI MACROCARPUM.

Large-fruited Grape Hyacinth.

Nat. Ord. LILIACEÆ.—LILYWORTS of Lindley.
Linnæan Class HEXANDRIA, Order MONOGYNIA.

MUSCARI, Tournefort.—Perianth corolline globoso-tubulose constricted at the mouth; limb very short six-toothed. *Stamens* six, inserted in the tube; filaments very short included. *Ovary* three celled; *ovules* few sub-horizontal anatropous; *style* short straight; *stigma* subtrigonal papillose. *Capsule* membranaceous, acutely triquetrous, three-celled, loculicidally three-valved. *Seeds* subglobose.

M. macrocarpum; perianth ventricose-cylindrical, contracted at the apex, four times longer than its stalk : scape compressed; leaves spreading, glaucous, elongate-lanceolate, acuminate concavely channelled.
M. macrocarpum, *Sweet in British Flower Garden,* t. 210.
M. moschatum, β. flavum, *Bot. Mag.*

The bulb is large, not rapidly increasing. The leaves, several of which are produced, spread in various directions, and are from six inches to a foot in length, lanceolate tapering to a very slender point, broadest at the base, convolutely concave, and channelled on the upper side, of a brownish glaucous colour, the margins tinged with purple. The scapes are erect, or declining a little from the weight of the flowers, flattened on each side, particularly on the inner one, smooth and glossy, of a bright purple, dotted with numerous minute green dots, terminating in a many-flowered raceme. The flowers which are of a bright blue tinged with purple before expansion, when expanded change to a bright yellow, and die off brown; deliciously fragrant. The bracts are very small, membranaceous, more or less lacerate; the pedicels very short and smooth, about four times shorter than the flowers. The perianth is tubular, with a contracted narrow mouth, bellied or ventricose towards the base, slightly six-furrowed, the mouth slightly six-crenate. The six stamens are inserted in the tube a little above the base on short filaments, flattened towards the base and tapering upwards; anthers dark purple. Ovary triangular, smooth, white; style short, smooth; stigma three-lobed. Capsule very large, of a greyish lilac or purple, with three broad flat sides.

Our drawing of this fragrant plant was taken in the beginning of May, at the nursery of Messrs. Whitley and Osborn, at Fulham. It had been received so long back as the year 1812 from Constantinople, from whence it was sent by Lady Liston, the lady of the British Ambassador to the Sublime Porte at that time; but as it increases slowly, it still continues a rare plant. It is a very desirable plant for all collections, both for its beauty and fragrance; and is certainly no variety of M. *moschatum*, with which it has been confused. The *Tibcadi Muscari* of the Dutch Florists, which this was supposed to be, proves to be nothing but the common M. *moschatum*.

The present species is said to be one of the principal flowers with which the Turkish females contrive to correspond in secret with their lovers, which renders it a plant of great value amongst them.

It thrives well in the open border of the flower-garden, in the common garden soil. The bulbs should be planted from four to six inches deep, according to their size; they will then flower every year regularly; but the plant is very slow of increase, except by seeds.

MUSCARI commutatum.

MUSCARI COMMUTATUM.

Dark-purple Grape Hyacinth.

———◆———

Nat. Ord. LILIACEÆ.—LILYWORTS of Lindley.
Linnæan Class HEXANDRIA, Order MONOGYNIA.

———

MUSCARI, Tournefort.—Perianth corolline globoso-tubulose constricted at the mouth; limb very short six-toothed. *Stamens* six, inserted in the tube; filaments very short included. *Ovary* three-celled; *ovules* few sub-horizontal anatropous; *style* short straight; *stigma* subtrigonal papillose. *Capsule* membranaceous, acutely triquetrous, three-celled, loculicidally three-valved. *Seeds* subglobose.

———

M. commutatum; raceme abbreviated; perianth ovate, the limb six-toothed connivent; leaves linear channelled flaccid.

M. commutatum, *Gussone. Pl. Rar.* x. 145. *Sweet Brit. Fl. Gard.* 2. s., t. 369.

Hyacinthus bifolius, *Gouan.*

———

The bulbs of this species are clustered, ovate, dark-brown. The scapes about half the length of the leaves, cylindrical, pale green. The leaves spreading, flaccid, about half a foot long, linear, paler and channelled above, dark-green, striated, and convex beneath, with the edges occasionally slightly ciliated. The flowers, about twenty in number, dark-purple scentless, are arranged in a short raceme. The pedicels are about a line in length, and together with the bracts, of a deep blue. The perianth is ovate, urceolate, furrowed, about two lines long, angular at the apex; its mouth closed by the six

270

connivent, blunt, segments. Stamens six very short, inclosed. Style white, about as long as the ovary. Capsule triangular, obcordate, deeply notched.

This pretty little bulbous plant is frequent in open, grassy meadows, in Italy and Sicily. It is near to *M. racemosum*, but in that the leaves are nearly filiform, and the perianth is longer, with the segments spreading, and the mouth consequently open. The specimens here figured were communicated to Professor Don by the Hon. W. T. H. Fox Strangways, from his collection at Abbotsbury Castle, Dorset, along with the following interesting particulars respecting its characters and history :—

" This species has probably been overlooked as a variety of either *M. racemosnm* or *botryoides*, to which at first sight it bears much resemblance. It is found in so many well known parts of Italy, that it is not likely to have been neglected on any other supposition. The leaves are almost precisely those of the smaller varieties of *M. racemosum*. Stalk pale-green, not growing darker towards the flowers, as in that species and *botryoides*. Corolla deep purple, almost black, mouth compressed, the obscure laciniæ always black, never dilute purple or white, nor expanding. Before opening, the closed mouths of the corollas are green, even while the other parts are becoming purple. Fruit triangular, heart-shaped. I have myself found this plant in Sicily, Apulia, the Campagna di Roma, and the pass called le gole d'Itri on the frontier of Rome and Naples, where it grows in company with the rare *Crocus suaveolens* of Bertoloni.

" It flowers in March and April. After many years cultivation, it has not varied in the least. Flowers scentless. Bulbs clustered. Plant low and small, except when sometimes drawn up among bushes."

The generic name alludes, according to Don, to the odour of the type of the group, and is from the Greek *moschos*, which again is derived from the Arabic word *misk*.

271

E.D.Smith Del.   MUSCARI *pallens*.

MUSCARI PALLENS.

Pale Grape Hyacinth.

Nat. Ord. LILIACEÆ.—LILYWORTS of Lindley.
Linnæan Class HEXANDRIA, Order MONOGYNIA.

MUSCARI, Tournefort,—Perianth corolline globoso-tubulose constricted at the mouth; limb very short six-toothed. *Stamens* six, inserted in the tube; filaments very short included. *Ovary* three-celled; *ovules* few sub-horizontal anatropous; *style* short straight; *stigma* subtrigonal, papillose. *Capsule* membranaceous, acutely triquetrous, three-celled, loculicidally three-valved. *Seeds* subglobose.

M. pallens; leaves linear acute glaucous smooth; raceme straight pyramidal; perianth congested inflato-cylindrical, the mouth open.

M. pallens, *Fischer Cat. Gorenk.* 1812, *p.* 9. *Sweet in Brit. Flow. Gard.* t. 259.

Hyacinthus pallens, *Marschal Bieberstein Taur. Cauc.* 1. *p.* 283.

The plant is bulbous, readily increasing by offsets. The leaves several together and quite smooth, glaucescent, linear acute, channelled on the inner side, striated at the back with numerous longitudinal lines, at first erect, but becoming more or less bent by their weight. The scapes are erect, smooth and glossy, more or less tinged with red or purple, particularly on those with the bluest flowers, terminated with a short pyramidical raceme of flowers, very much crowded or squeezed together, the flowers nodding, very pale blue, or white tinged

271

with blue, exceedingly fragrant. The bracts small, scale-like, white, two or three at the base of the very short pedicles. The perianth is tubular, nearly cylindrical, but a little inflated, the mouth spreading widely open, not nearly closed as in M. *botryoides*; slightly divided at the mouth into six short, broadish, rounded segments, that are a little reflexed. Stamens six, inserted in the tube; filaments short, smooth, slender towards the point, and inserted into the back of the anthers; anthers purple, two-lobed. Ovary three-sided, glaucescent; style short, smooth; stigma a simple blunt point.

A very pretty spring-flowering bulb, native of Tauria and Caucasus, and flowering in our borders in April and May. It was first introduced to the Apothecaries' Garden at Chelsea, where it had been received from Dr. Fischer. It is delightfully fragrant as well as pretty, and two or three flowering stems are produced from the same bulb in succession. It is nearest related to M. *botryoides*, but its flowers are more cylindrical, much more expanded at the mouth, and they are crowded together.

A light sandy soil in the open border suits it best, to be planted from four to six inches deep, according to the size of the bulbs, which are quite hardy, and are readily increased by offsets from the roots. They may also be grown in pots, which can be removed into the house when in flower, for the sake of their fragrance, but the flowers will not be so fine in pots, as those in the open ground.

Muscari is, according to some, a name derived from the Latin, and signifies the top of a herb, wherein the seed lieth. It is also used for a fly-flap, to kill or drive away flies, the head of flowers on the simple stem not being very unlike something of that kind.

272

E D Smith del.   MUSCARI botryoides.   A Gurley sculp.

MUSCARI BOTRYOIDES.

Common Grape Hyacinth.

Nat. Ord. LILIACEÆ.—LILYWORTS of Lindley.
Linnæan Class HEXANDRIA, Order MONOGYNIA.

MUSCARI, Tournefort.—*Perianth* corolline globoso-tubulose constricted at the mouth ; limb very short six-toothed. *Stamens* six, inserted in the tube : filaments very short included. *Ovary* three-celled ; *ovules* few sub-horizontal anatropous ; *style* short straight ; *stigma* subtrigonal, papillose. *Capsule* membranaceous, acutely triquetrous, three-celled, loculicidally three-valved. *Seeds* subglobose.

M. botryoides ; perianth globose uniform, the lower flowers more remote ; leaves straight linear narrowed at the base, channelled.
Muscari botryoides, *Miller. Sweet in Brit. Fl. Gard.* t. 15.
Hyacinthus botryoides, *Willd. Sp. Pl.* ii. *p.* 170.
    α. *azureum,* flowers azure. (fig. a.)
    β. *pallidum,* flowers pallid. (fig. c.)
    γ. *album,* flowers white. (fig. b.)

The plant is bulbous, the bulbs increasing rapidly by numerous offsets. The leaves, several together, are smooth, erect linear channelled, bluntish, narrowest at the base. The scapes are generally two from the same bulb, erect, about the length of the leaves, smooth, round on one side, and flat on the other, slightly angular. The flowers grow in a crowded cluster, globular, all of the same form, the lowermost farthest apart, nodding. Bracts two, at the base of the peduncle, one on

272

each side, very short, succulent. The peduncles are cylindrical, shorter than the flowers, more than double the length of the bracts. The perianth is globular, the mouth contracted and terminated in six slight marginated notches. Stamens six, inserted in the middle of the tube; filaments widest at the base, and narrowing upwards; anthers cordate, incumbent, two-celled. Ovary triangular. Style about the length of the stamens.

The three varieties represented in the accompanying plate are very desirable plants for adorning the flower-borders in spring, where they may be planted in patches in conspicuous situations, either mixed together, or separate, according to the taste of the cultivator. The pale blue variety is the least common, and perhaps is the most beautiful.

They all increase rapidly by offsets from the bulbs, and thrive well in a rich light soil, flowering in April, some time before M. *racemosum.*

273

CORBULARIA tenuifolia.

CORBULARIA TENUIFOLIA.

Slender-leaved Hoop-petticoat.

Nat. Ord. AMARYLLIDACEÆ.—AMARYLLIDS of Lindley.
Linnæan Class HEXANDRIA, Order MONOGYNIA.

CORBULARIA, Haworth.—*Perianth* superior, tubulose; the tube funnel-shaped; segments of the limb narrow, spreading, suberect, much shorter than the coronet. *Crown* or *coronet* large funnel-shaped truncate, longer than the tube. *Style* and *filaments* declined, recurved; *anthers* short, attached at the middle incumbent, versatile; *filaments* successively matured, the sepaline adhering to the tube near the base, the petaline inserted at the base. *Ovary* subturbinate cylindrical, three-celled, three-valved; *ovules* numerous.

C. tenuifolia; leaves semicylindrical shining, erect after flowering; crown deeply six-lobed, the lobes rounded; style much exserted.
C. tenuifolia, *Salisbury in. Trans. Hort. Soc.* i. 349.
Narcissus tenuifolius, *Salisbury Prodr.* 222. *Sweet's Brit. Flow. Gard.* t. 114.

The bulb in this species is rather small. The leaves, several upon the bulb, are spreading slender semicylindrical slightly furrowed on the upper side, dark green, smooth and glossy, from nine to twelve inches in length, and about a line broad. The scape is smooth, slightly angular, four to six inches long, one-flowered, and having a membranaceous wrinkled spathe, split on one side nearly half way down, and ending in a sharpish point. The perianth is funnel-shaped; the tube green. channelled with six deep furrows, narrow at the base and widening upwards, or obpyramidal; the segments of the limb six, very short and narrow, acute, erect or slightly curved inwards, pale yellow, shorter than the tube, and decurrent down it. The coronet is a bright yellow, very large, bell-shaped. rugged and plaited, six-lobed, the lobes regular, and rounded. The six stamens are inserted in the tube; their filaments long and slender, but shorter than the coronet, with the points ascending; their anthers incumbent, with yellow pollen. The style is smooth, longer than the coronet, and exserted beyond it; stigma deeply and unequally three-lobed, the lobes spreading, fimbriate.

This rare and beautiful plant, was figured from plants which bloomed in the Apothecaries' Garden at Chelsea. It blooms in the latter end of April. The species is readily distinguished from N. *Bulbocodium* by its deeply six-lobed crown and slender leaves; it also comes in bloom earlier than that species, and appears to be equally hardy. The plant thrives well in the open border, in common garden soil; but better if planted in a soil composed of light sandy loam, in which it both grows and blooms stronger. The only method of increasing it, is by the offsets of its roots, or by seeds which sometimes ripen.

The name is derived from *corbula* a little basket, in reference to the shape of the coronet.

74

E.D.smith del.

CORBULARIA serotina.

CORBULARIA SEROTINA.

Late flowering Hoop-petticoat.

Nat. Ord. AMARYLLIDACEÆ.—AMARYLLIDS of Lindley.
Linnæan Class HEXANDRIA, Order MONOGYNIA.

CORBULARIA, Haworth.—Perianth superior, tubulose ; the tube funnel-shaped ; segments of the limb narrow, spreading, suberect, much shorter than the coronet. *Crown* or *coronet* large funnel-shaped truncate, longer than the tube. *Style* and *filaments* declined, recurved ; *anthers* short, attached at the middle incumbent versatile ; *filaments* successively matured, the sepaline adhering to the tube near the base, the petaline inserted at the base. *Ovary* subturbinate cylindrical, three-celled, three-valved ; *ovules* numerous.

C. *serotina;* leaves semicylindrical elongate dark green twisted semistriate flattish above ; coronet turgid truncate entire rugulose ; style as long as the filaments, included.

C. serotina, *Haworth Mon. Narcis.* p. 1. *Sweet Brit. Flow. Gard.* 2. *s.,* t. 164.

Narcissus turgidus, *Salisb. prod.* 222.

Narcissus Bulbocodium, *Bot. Mag.* t. 88 ; not of *Linnæus* herb.

In this species the bulb is small, rounded at the bottom, and tapering towards the leaves, covered by a very thin pale brown skin. The leaves, two three or four from each bulb, taper to a long slender point ; they are sometimes a foot and

274

a half in length, bent and twisted in various directions, of a very dark green semicylindrical, striated at the back, flat on the upper surface, and slightly channelled. The scapes are six inches high slightly flattened, bearing a membranaceous spathe, tubular at the base, which is split in the upper part and tapering to an acute point. The tube of the perianth is narrow at the base, and inflated gradually upwards; the segments of the limb six, narrow, about half an inch in length, tapering to a point, green down the back, the edges yellow. The crown is about three-fourths of an inch in length, of a bright yellow, gradually spreading, and becoming wider to the top, where it is about half an inch across; it is marked with several deepish channels, which make it rather uneven at the top, and rigid inside, and at the apex is entire, not lobed or crenate. The tube and crown together measure an inch and a half in length. Stamens six, the filaments inserted in the base of the perianth, declining, the anthers incumbent, versatile, curved. Ovary somewhat turbinate, cylindrical, three-celled, three-valved; the ovules numerous, disposed in four rows; style about the length of the stamens, at first declining, but ascending at the end; stigma capitate.

This plant flowers in May, a month later than the allied forms of the common hoop-petticoat. It grows wild on the Pyrenees.

The *Corbularias* being natives of the South of Europe chiefly, require slight protection in severe winters. They thrive best in a light loamy soil, and a sheltered situation; but also succeed well in pots, if treated as bulbous frame plants. The present species, if occasionally transplanted when the bulbs are quiescent, succeeds also in the open ground. It is the hardiest of the group.

NARCISSUS Trewianus

NARCISSUS TREWIANUS.

Bazelman Major Narcissus.

———•———

Nat. Ord. AMARYLLIDACEÆ.—AMARYLLIDS of Lindley.
Linnæan Class HEXANDRIA, Order MONOGYNIA.

———

NARCISSUS, Linnæus.—*Perianth* superior, salver-shaped; tube subcylindrical straight; limb six-parted, the lobes equal spreading or reflexed. *Crown* (or nectary or cup) funnel-shaped bell-shaped or rotate, entire or lobed, shorter or longer than the tube. *Stamens* six, inserted in two rows at the summit of the tube of the perianth below the crown, included; *filaments* very short, free or adherent to the tube; *anthers* oblong incumbent. *Ovary* inferior three-celled; *ovules* numerous in the central angle of the cells in many rows, horizontal anatropous; *style* thread-like; *stigma* obtuse. *Capsule* membranous obtusely three-sided, three-celled, loculicidally three-valved. *Seeds* numerous or few, somewhat globular with a black-wrinkled testa.

Sect. HERMIONE.—Style straight slender; filaments conniving, with a short curved point, alternately inserted, the sepaline at the mouth of the tube decurrent; anthers after inversion acute-oval incumbent versatile. Capsule erect. Tube slender cylindrical, enlarged at the mouth; crown shorter than the tube or limb.

———

Λ. *Trewianus;* umbels many-flowered: segments of the perianth ovate shortly mucronulate at the apex, at first imbricate, afterwards subreflexed-tortuous; tube shorter than the limb, crown nearly twice as short as the segments, lobato-crenulate, plicato-corrugate.

N. Trewianus, *Ker Bot. Mag.* t. 1298.
N. orientalis, a. *Bot. Mag.* t. 940.
N. grandiflorus, *Haworth Syn. Succ.* 332.
Hermione grandiflora, *Haworth Supp. Succ.* 141.
Hermione crenularis, *Salisbury Trans. Hort. Soc.* 1. 263.
Hermione Trewiana, *Sweet Brit. Flow. Gard.* t. 118.
H. brevistyla var Trewiana, *Herb. Amaryll.* 324.

———

275

The bulb of this fine Narcissus, is rounder than in related species. The leaves from two to four in number, from six to eight inches long when not forced, tapering upwards, and ending in rather a bluntish point, furrowed on the upper side keeled below, longitudinally striated, and somewhat glaucescent. The scape is longer than the leaves, very stout and succulent, solid below, but hollow from about the middle, subcompressed, with a sharp angle on each side, striated longitudinally, a little glaucescent or mealy. The spathe is ovate, acute, membranaceous. The umbels are four- to eight-flowered, most frequently six-flowered. The tube of the perianth bluntly triangular, about half as long again as the segments of the limb, which are ovate, tapering to the base, white, every other one terminated by a short mucrone, the others ending in a small callosity; when first expanded, they are flat and closely imbricate; but at length they become more or less twisted. The crown is about one-fourth of an inch in height, nearly three-fourths of an inch across, rugulose, and crenulated at the margin, golden yellow. Stamens six, inserted in the mouth of the tube; three extending beyond it, and three equal to it. Style smooth, flat, and slightly furrowed on two sides; stigma of three short rounded lobes, slightly reflexed at the points, and pustulose.

This is one of the most common and beautiful of the Narcissi, sold in the seed-shops, and requires only the ordinary treatment of Hyacinths and other Dutch bulbs.

276

NARCISSUS *pulchellus*

NARCISSUS PULCHELLUS.

White-cupped Ganymede Narcissus.

———

Nat. Ord. AMARYLLIDACEÆ.—AMARYLLIDS of Lindley.
Linnæan Class HEXANDRIA, Order MONOGYNIA.

———

NARCISSUS, Linnæus.—*Perianth* superior, salver-shaped; tube subcylindrical straight; limb six-parted, the lobes equal spreading or reflexed. *Crown* (or nectary or cup) funnel-shaped bell-shaped or rotate, entire or lobed, shorter or longer than the tube. *Stamens* six inserted in two rows at the summit of the tube of the perianth below the crown, included; *filaments* very short, free or adherent to the tube; *anthers* oblong incumbent. *Ovary* inferior three-celled; *ovules* numerous in the central angle of the cells in many rows, horizontal anatropous; *style* thread-like; *stigma* obtuse. *Capsule* membranous obtusely three-sided, three-celled, loculicidally three-valved. *Seeds* numerous or few, somewhat globular with a black wrinkled testa.

Sect. GANYMEDES.—Style straight slender; filaments adhering to the upper part of the tube, with diversity; sepaline stamens much prolonged. Limb decidedly reflex; cup equalling or shorter than the limb; tube slender drooping. Capsule erect.

———

N. pulchellus; leaves erect linear subsemicylindrical channelled above striate; segments of the perianth as long as the tube reflexed lanceolate; crown shorter poculiform repand; style included.
N. pulchellus, *Salisbury Prodr.* 223.
N. triandrus var. luteus, *Bot. Mag.* t. 1262.
Ganymedes pulchellus, *Salisbury Trans. Hort. Soc.* i. 354.   *Sweet Brit. Flow. Gard.* 2. s., t. 99.

———

The bulb is round, about the size of a blackbird's egg, clothed with a thin pale brown membranaceous skin. The leaves are narrowly linear, acute semicylindrical, striated with pro-
276

minent longitudinal lines, channelled on the upper side, dark green, smooth, about the length of the scape which is erect, cylindrical, smooth, from six to nine inches in height having a one-valved, membranaceous, lanceolate, acute, one to four flowered spathe. The perianth is tubular, crowned, the crown surrounded by six petal-like leaflets or segments; the tube is about eleven lines long, bluntly triangular, slender at the base, and becoming gradually inflated upwards; the segments of the limb are elliptically oblong, cuspidate at the points, pale yellow, all reflexed somewhat twisted, about the length of the tube or sometimes scarcely so long, and about twice the length of the crown. The crown is bowl-shaped, white or slightly tinged with straw-colour, slightly crenulate or undulate. There are six stamens of which three are inserted about half way up the tube, and the other three are inserted at the mouth of the tube, on longish filaments, that are connected to the back of the anthers, the three lower ones being on short filaments. The style is smooth, slender; the stigma three-lobed, the lobes pustulose. The ovary is three-celled, three-valved, with numerous ovules in each cell, disposed in four rows.

The present and some other species have been thought to differ from *Narcissus*, in the leaflets of the perianth being reflexed; in having three of the stamens inserted a long way down the tube, and the other three in the mouth, in the ovary bearing two septa up each cell, each of which bear two rows of seeds, the seeds being rounded. The divisions however which have been proposed in this genus do not seem to have generic value, and have not been generally adopted.

The Ganymedean group of Narcissus consist of species which are very delicate, and produce elegant flowers, none of them more beautiful than the present, with its delicate pale yellow leaflets and straw-coloured or almost pure white crown.

It is well deserving a place in all collections, as it will thrive well in any rich light soil, and increases readily by offsets, and by seeds.

The name *Narcissus*, is by some said to come from *narke* stupor; in allusion to the effect of the odour of the flowers on the nervous system.

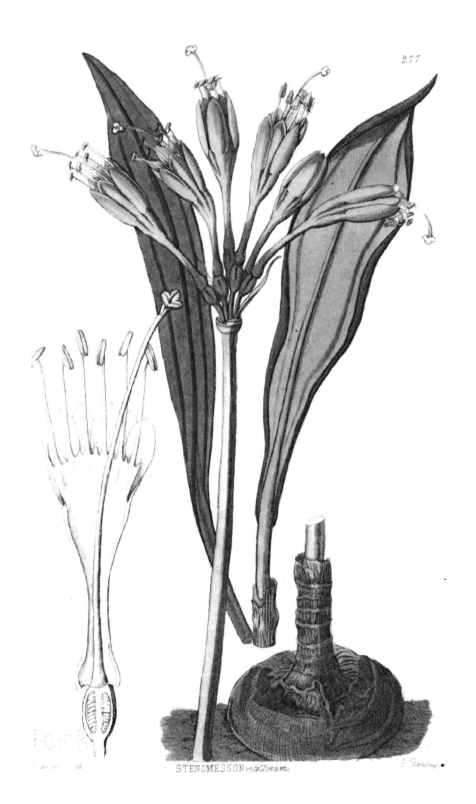

STENOMESSON *vitellinum.*

STENOMESSON VITELLINUM.

Yolk-of-Egg Stenomesson.

Nat. Ord. AMARYLLIDACEÆ.—AMARYLLIDS of Lindley.
Linnæan Class HEXANDRIA, Order MONOGYNIA.

STENOMESSON, Herbert.—*Perianth* superior corolline; the tube constricted in the middle, wider upwards, a little curved; limb short, regular; crown short. *Stamens* six; filaments straight connected by a membrane; anthers striate incumbent. *Style* straight, before maturity sloping; *Stigma* dilated. *Capsule* broad ovate, three-furrowed, three-celled, three-lobed. *Seeds* black, obliquely oblong.

S. vitellinum; leaves obovate-oblong three-nerved, petiolate, the margin revolute, glaucous beneath, produced after the flowers; umbels six-flowered; segments of the perianth erect; teeth of the cup obtuse undivided; stamens exserted.

S. vitellinum, *Lindley in Bot. Reg.* 1843, t. 2.

A very pretty bulbous plant, having the bulbs placenta-shaped, constricted at the neck. The flowers are produced after the leaves, on a glaucous scape about a span high. The leaves are obovate-oblong with a revolute margin, stalked and three-nerved. The flowers are about six together in an umbel, erect, on stalks shorter than themselves, and of a deep rich yellow colour. The alternate stamens are shorter than the rest. The stigma is three-lobed and capitate.

This plant ranks among the prettiest of the Western American bulbs; but is at present extremely rare. It is a native of Lima, whence it was sent by John Maclean, Esq. to the Horticultural Society of London with whom it flowered in February 1842. The yellow flowers, and their general appearance, recall to mind the yellow *Calostemmas* of New Holland; only they are larger.

It is essentially distinguished from the other known species by its broad leaves, depressed bulbs, and the intermediate teeth of the cup being obtuse and undivided.

The plant requires to be grown in a cool stove. It should be kept warm and moist while growing, but cooler and drier while at rest; and should have a sandy loamy soil. It is increased by offsets.

Stenomesson comes from *stenos* narrow, and *messon* middle; alluding to the constricted form of the perianth.

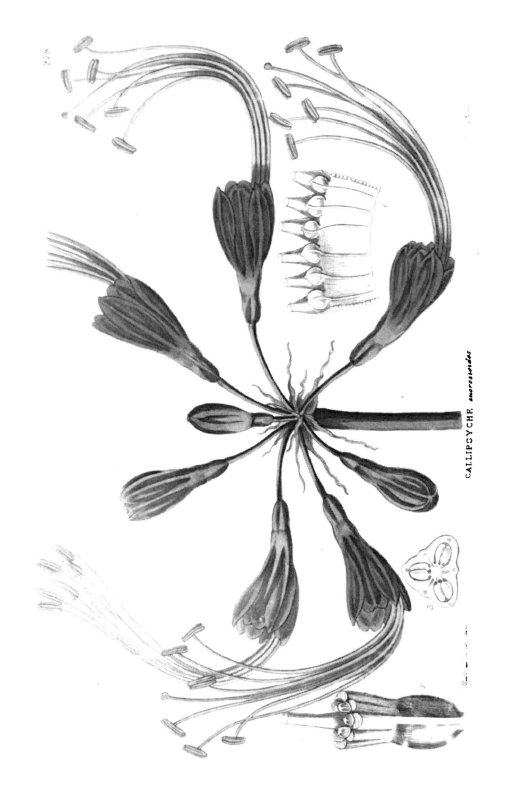

CALLIPSYCHE. *amaryllioides*

CALLIPSYCHE EUCROSIOIDES.

Two-coloured Fairy-bloom.

Nat. Ord. AMARYLLIDACEÆ.—AMARYLLIDS of Lindley.
Linnæan Class HEXANDRIA, Order MONOGYNIA.

CALLIPSYCHE, Herbert.—*Perianth* superior corolline, declined, laterally compressed, the segments connate into a short tube, regular; sepals boat-shaped broader than the petals somewhat reflexed at the apex; petals clasping the genitals. *Stamens* six, filaments free inserted in the mouth of the tube, terete, very long, tuberculate at the base; anthers versatile affixed by the base. *Ovary* three-celled; *ovules* numerous in two rows; *style* deflexed; *stigma* capitate.

C. *eucrosioides;* bulbs roundish; leaves few; scape ten-flowered terete glaucous; peduncles equal; tube green, declined, mellifluous; petals obtuse; filaments unequal the lowest longest.
C. eucrosioides, *Herbert in Bot. Reg.* 1842, *misc.* 49; and 1845, t. 45.

This is a handsome bulb, having roundish bulbs. The leaves, few in number, are green, with a blade a foot long, and about four inches wide, a good deal tessellated and pitted. The scape bears ten flowers, glaucous, tapering, smaller upwards, and is about two and a half feet high. The spathe and bracts soon wither. The peduncles are green, equal, about an inch long. The tube of the perianth is green, curved downwards, scarcely a quarter of an inch long, full of honey; the limb scarlet, scarcely an inch long, with obtuse petals. The stamens are pale green; the filaments rarely five inches long, unequal, the lowest the most extended, the style is about the same length. The ovary is oblong, three-cornered with three furrows, green, its cells each containing about twenty-three ovules.

278

This very curious bulb was flowered at Spofforth in April 1844, and appears to be still very rare. The late Dean of Manchester stated it to have been brought from St. Blas or S. Felipe on the west coast of Mexico. It seems to like shade and heat, and flowers without leaves in the spring.

The genus is regarded as an ally of Eucrosia, because of the tubercles in its orifice. The Fig. 1, represents the tube of the flower with the base of the filaments, and the six tubercles of the orifice; 2, the ovary, tube of the flower, and tubercles *in situ*; 3, a transverse section of the ovary.

The bulbs should be potted in sandy loam and leaf-mould. In summer, while growing, it requires to be kept in a temperature of 75° or 80° by day, and shaded in sunny weather. In autumn the leaves will naturally die off, when it should be kept in a warm greenhouse, quite dry, for a few weeks. As soon as the scape makes its appearance, which will be in spring, water should again be given gradually, and the heat increased. It must be increased by seeds or offsets.

279

PLACEA *ornata*

PLACEA ORNATA.

Gay-flowered Placea.

———

Nat. Ord. AMARYLLIDACEÆ.—AMARYLLIDS of Lindley.
Linnæan Class HEXANDRIA, Order MONOGYNIA.

———

PLACEA, Miers.—Perianth petaloid, epigynous, subdeclinate, six-parted; tube none; limb equal linear-oblong spathulate mucronate at the apex, spreading-reflexed, the two lower broadly divaricate; crown six-leaved, very much declinate, its segments suberect, rising from the epigynous disk, linear-spathulate, keeled behind, emarginate at the apex. *Stamens* six; filaments much declined, adscendent above, about half as long as the perianth, three of them somewhat longer; anthers obovate. *Ovary* inferior, three-cornered, three-celled; *style* simple declinate incurved at the apex; *stigma* gibbose-clavate, obtuse, hollow.

———

P. ornata; perianth thickish, white, the segments spathulate-oblong, mucronate at the apex, marked with four vermilion lines of which the outer ones are semipinnate; crown white, crimson at the apex; leaves linear, smooth, bluntly keeled beneath.

P. ornata, *Miers in litt;* and in *Bot. Reg.* 1841, t. 50.

———

"This very elegant plant," writes Mr. Miers, " was found by me in the year 1824, in one of the lateral branches of the lofty chain of the Andes that jut into the plain of Aconcagua. The scape, rising to the height of nine inches, bears a head of four to seven flowers, upon pedicels from two to three inches long, or rarely by abortion it is one-flowered. The marcescent linear spathe bears within it as many membranaceous bracts

279

as there are flowers. The separation of the two lower segments appears at first sight as if two of them had been torn away. The flowers externally are snow-white, the colour of the brilliant vermilion lines being in no degree distinguishable on the back of the segments, where they are also pure white and striated longitudinally. The filaments are of a pale crimson, and the anthers, somewhat emarginate at the base, are versatile. The stamens and coronet originate outside of a raised epigynous disc, together with the perianth. The style is somewhat longer than the stamens, and more declinate, but the apex is curved upwards to meet the anthers, as in the genus *Amaryllis*. I gathered a number of the bulbs of this beautiful plant, which I regret were all lost by shipwreck, together with the greater part of my collections."

From an examination of a dried specimen given by Mr. Miers to Dr. Lindley, the latter is inclined to think that the coronet is not composed of six distinct lobes, as Mr. Miers regards it, but that they are united into a cup about one-fourth of their whole length. In the opinion of the Dean of Manchester, the genus is most nearly allied to *Eucrosia*.

The accompanying figure was made by Mr. Miers from the fresh plant, of which nothing further seems known.

ANIGOSANTHOS *Manglesii.*

ANIGOZANTHOS MANGLESII.

Mr. Mangles's Anigozanthos.

———

Nat. Ord. Hæmodoraceæ.—Blood-roots of Lindley.
Linnæan Class Hexandria, Order Monogynia.

———

ANIGOZANTHOS, Labillardiere.—Perianth superior coloured tubulose, with a woolly covering of branched hairs ; limb six-cleft, segments subequal secund, long persistent. *Stamens* six, inserted in the throat, adscendent ; *anthers* erect. *Ovary* three-celled, the cells many-seeded ; *style* filiform deciduous ; *stigma* simple. *Capsule* three-celled, dehiscing at the apex. *Seeds* numerous.

———

A. Manglesii ; stem clothed with persistent velvety down ; anthers mutic, five times as long as the filaments ; stigmas capitate.
A. Manglesii, D. Don. in Sweet Brit. Fl. Gard. 2. s., t. 265.

———

A beautiful tufted growing perennial plant of peculiar character. The leaves are uniform, erect, of a glaucous green, glabrous, even and entire at the edges, terminated by a sharp, brown, rigid point, varying from half a foot to eighteen inches in height; and from half an inch to an inch in breadth. The stem is erect, branched, cylindrical, from two to three feet high, clothed with a short thick crimson persistent down resembling velvet and composed of branched hairs. The flowers are arranged in short, terminal, spiked racemes, on very short,

280

round peduncles which as well as the base of the perianth is clothed with crimson down. The perianth is tubular, cylindrical, two or three inches long, often splitting longitudinally, thickly covered with short branched hairs of a green colour, except at the base, which is slightly swollen and rounded, and at the limb where they assume a yellow tint; the limb is erect, white above, divided into six ovate-lanceolate pointed equal segments, frequently united in pairs. The stamens six in number are equal, inserted into the mouth of the tube, the free portion very short, glabrous flat and dilated towards the base; the anthers linear, blunt, slightly recurved orange, five times longer than the free portion of the filaments. The ovary is globular, three-celled, slightly adherent to the tube of the perianth, the ovules numerous in each cell, attached to a longitudinal placenta; the style slender, filiform, glabrous; the stigma capitate, projecting considerably beyond the mouth of the tube.

This singularly beautiful species of *Anigozanthos* was raised in the garden of Robert Mangles, Esq. from seeds brought from Swan River by Sir James Stirling. The seeds were sown in August. The young plants were potted, and kept in an airy part of the greenhouse during winter. Early in the spring they were repotted, and in April planted out in a border composed of loam, leaf mould, and bog earth, in equal proportions, with a slight mixture of pounded chalk, in which the plants were found to thrive amazingly, shewing flower at the age of ten months. In bog earth alone, they do not thrive so well. A cold frame will protect them sufficiently in the winter. The slugs are very fond of the leaves. The plant affords offsets freely, and is therefore easily multiplied. The greater length of the anthers, and the capitate stigma, essentially distinguish it from the rest of the genus.

The generic name refers to the flowers being elevated on a tall naked stem.

281

ANIGOSANTHOS flavida

ANIGOZANTHUS FLAVIDA.

Yellow-haired Anigozanthus.

———◆———

Nat. Ord. HÆMODORACEÆ.—BLOOD-ROOTS of Lindley.
Linnæan Class HEXANDRIA, Order MONOGYNIA.

———

ANIGOZANTHOS, Labillardiere.—*Perianth* superior coloured tubulose, with a woolly covering of branched hairs; limb six-cleft, segments subequal secund, long persistent. *Stamens* six, inserted in the throat, adscendent; *anthers* erect. *Ovary* three-celled, the cells many-seeded; *style* filiform deciduous; *stigma* simple. *Capsule* three-celled, dehiscing at the apex. *Seeds* numerous.

———

A. flavida; stem and foliage smooth; panicle stiff, its branches clothed with deciduous tomentum; limb of the perianth nearly equal spreading; anthers with a reflexed apiculus.

A. flavida, *Redoute Liliaceæ,* 176. *Bot. Reg.* 1838, t. 37.
A. grandiflora, *Salisbury,* ex *Steudel.*
Schwägrichenia flavida, *Spreng. Syst. Veg.* ii. 26.

———

This is a very curious and interesting plant. The stem grows a foot and a half high, and is branched at the apex where it is clothed with deciduous greenish yellow, sometimes purplish, tomentum. The flowers are tubular, swollen at the base, with a narrow curved tube widening somewhat upwards, the short segments of the limb turned upwards; they are clothed with greenish yellow wool intermixed with purplish hairs. The anthers are fixed in the throat of the perianth on filaments about half as long as the segments of the limb. The singular short branched hairs with which the perianth, and upper part of the stem are clothed, render them extremely interesting when in flower.

This species was introduced into our gardens from the South Coast of New Holland, where it appears to be of common occurrence; nevertheless we seldom see it, although a fine showy plant and of very curious structure. That form which is here represented, is not precisely the same as that generally cultivated, and inhabits a rather different country, having been obtained from the Swan River Colony by Robert Mangles, Esq. It is of more robust growth, and instead of being whole-coloured it has a dash of brown-purple on the upper ramifications of the panicle. Another form represented in the *Botanical Magazine*, has a purple lining to the flower, and a dark purple stem. The species in fact varies in regard to the colour of its surface, in a remarkable manner. It sometimes has brilliant scarlet and green flowers.

The figure 1. represents the ovary, from which the perianth has been cut off; 2. is a vertical section of the same part; 3. is one of the hairs that clothe the surface of the flowers.

The plant is a greenhouse perennial. The soil best suited to it is a rich loam, mixed with about one-fourth of sand and peat, to which a small quantity of dung should be added. To grow it well, it is necessary to give it plenty of pot-room, and to place it in an open airy part of the greenhouse, near the glass. When growing luxuriantly, it requires a good supply of water, and should be well syringed over-head. If planted out in a border, in summer, it will grow much better than when confined in a pot, and is, probably, sufficiently hardy, with a little protection, to withstand the winter in the milder parts of England. Its propagation is extremely simple, as it throws out young shoots freely from its sides.

ANIGOZANTHUS FLAVIDA;
var. BICOLOR.

Two-coloured Anigozanthus.

———◆———

Nat. Ord. Hæmodoraceæ.—Blood Roots of Lindley.
Linnæan Class Hexandria, Order Monogynia.

———————

ANIGOZANTHOS, Labillardiere.—*Perianth* superior coloured tubulose, with a woolly covering of branched hairs; limb six-cleft, segments subequal secund, long persistent. *Stamens* six, inserted in the throat, adscendent; *anthers* erect. *Ovary* three-celled, the cells many-seeded; *style* filiform deciduous; *stigma* simple. *Capsule* three-celled, dehiscing at the apex. *Seeds* numerous.

———————

A. flavida; stem and foliage smooth, the panicle stiff, its branches clothed with deciduous tomentum; limb of the perianth nearly equal spreading; anthers with a reflexed apiculus.

A. flavida; *see* t. 281.

Var. *bicolor;* leaves broader, perianth very much branched; ovary scarlet, tube of the perianth green.

A. flavida, var. bicolor, *Lindley in Bot. Reg.* 1838, t. 64.

———————

This is a very beautiful variety of the species, another form of which is represented at t. 281. It is indeed strikingly beautiful and deserves the particular notice of the cultivators of ornamental plants. Scarlet and green are not often intermingled in the flowers of plants; and when they are, the union is not

282

always agreeable. In this instance, however, the two are so harmoniously blended and softened together, probably on account of the tomentum which clothes the surface, that a singularly rich velvet-like effect is the result. *A. Manglesii*, as well as this, varies in colour, some plants having the flowers all green, and others having them two-coloured, which is the common garden state.

The panicle in the variety here represented is much more divaricating than in *A. flavida*, but it possesses no distinctive character except that of colour.

The fig. 1. represents a transverse section of an ovary; 2. the ovary, style, and stigma; 3. one of the curious branched hairs much magnified.

These plants are increased by seeds which should be sown in light soil, and placed in a cool pit or frame. The best time to sow the seeds is early in autumn or in spring. The plant may also be multiplied by taking off the side shoots, which will root freely in sand. It must have plenty of pot-room, and a considerable quantity of water when it is growing luxuriantly. If cultivated in a greenhouse it should be placed in a light and airy situation, but it will succeed very well if planted out in a pit which is sufficiently protected during winter. The best soil for potting is a rich loam, mixed with peat and sand.

ALLIUM *neapolitanum*

ALLIUM NEAPOLITANUM.

Neapolitan Moly.

———

Nat. Ord. LILIACEÆ.—LILYWORTS of Lindley.
Linnæan Class HEXANDRIA, Order MONOGYNIA.

————

ALLIUM, Linnæus.—Perianth regular, inferior, six-parted, the three inner segments smaller. *Stamens* six; filaments awl-shaped, more or less flattened, about as long as the corolla; anthers incumbent. *Ovary* superior, turbinate; style simple; *stigma* undivided. *Capsule* short broad, three-lobed, three-celled, the cells one, two, or rarely many-seeded, three-valved, the valves with central partitions. *Seeds* few roundish angular.

————

A. neapolitanum; leaves lorate-lanceolate, keeled; spathe one-valved short; umbels many-flowered; segments of the perianth oblong obtuse; stamens half as long as the perianth.

A. neapolitanum, *Cyrill Pl. Rar. Neap.* i. 13. *Sweet Brit. Fl. Gard.* t. 201.

A. album, *Savi App.* i. 352.

A. lacteum, *Sibthorp. Flor. Græc.* t. 325.

————

A showy plant, with oblong proliferous bulbs. The leaves two or three in number are lanceolate-linear, acute, channelled on the upper side, bluntly keeled underneath, striate, smooth and glossy. The scape is longer than the leaves, slightly three-sided, smooth and shining. The umbel is many-flowered, drooping before expansion, and when expanded a little nodding; the spathe bursting on one side, cordate acute, thin and mem-

283

branaceous when the flowers are expanded. The flowers are from twelve to twenty in number, loosely spreading, on long and slender pedicels. The perianth is divided nearly to the base, into six leaflets, which are oblong-ovate, obtuse, toothed at the points, the three outer ones rather the largest, pure white, with a strong nerve down the middle of each. The six stamens are inserted in the base of the leaflets; the filaments subulate flat dilated downwards, about half the length of the perianth; the anthers incumbent; the pollen pale yellow. The style is smooth, tinged with red, about the length of the stamens; the stigma slightly three-lobed. Ovary three-celled. Seeds few, smooth, nearly globular.

Our drawing of this handsome and fragrant species was made at the Nursery of the late Mr. Colvill. It flowers in spring. The species is a native of the South of Europe.

Being a native of the warmer parts of Europe, it is rather more tender than some other species of *Allium*; it therefore requires a warm border, and to be planted about six inches deep, to be out of the reach of frost. A light sandy soil suits it best; and it increases freely by offsets at the root.

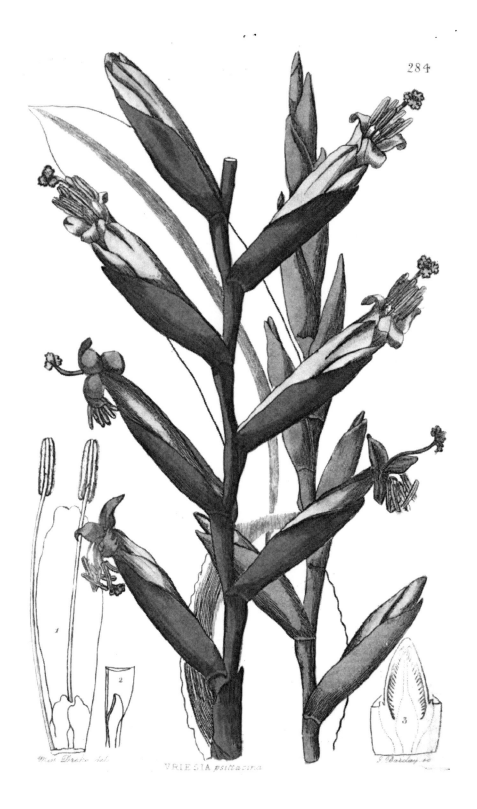

284

VRIESIA *psittacina*

VRIESIA PSITTACINA.

Parrot-flowered Vriesia.

Nat. Ord. BROMELIACEÆ.—BROMELWORTS of Lindley.
Linnæan Class HEXANDRIA, Order MONOGYNIA.

VRIESIA, Lindley.—Perianth six-leaved, the sepals convolute, equal, shorter than the petals which are revolute at the points; petals bearing two semiadnate undivided scales. *Stamens* exserted, three inserted in the base of the petals free, three inserted within the petals and connate at the base; anthers linear plane. *Ovary* semi-inferior conical; *stigma* three-lobed, the lobes convolute and sinuate villose.

V. psittacina; leaves oblong acute dilated at the base; sepals somewhat shorter than the petals; stamens exserted.
V. psittacina, *Lindley in Bot. Reg.* 1843, t. 10.
Tillandsia psittacina, *Hooker Bot. Mag.* t. 2841.

This is a very showy stove perennial with flat erect leaves, and a scape bearing two-ranked distant flowers, having large channelled scarlet bracts. The flowers themselves are yellow tube-like from the convolution of the sepals. The petals are longer than the sepals and turned back at the points.

"Although," observes Dr. Lindley, writing in 1843, "the limits of the genera of the Bromeliaceous order are much better defined than they were a few years ago, there are no doubt some distinct groups still concealed among the little known species crowded together under the name of *Tillandsia.*

284

The present instance we conceive to be one of them. Although referred to *Tillandsia* this has neither a superior ovary, nor the scaleless petals that are essential to that genus. On the contrary, it evidently belongs to Endlicher's second section of the order, at present consisting of *Pitcairnia* and *Brocchinia* only; from the latter it differs in its revolute scaled petals, and distinct filaments; from the latter in its distinct sepals, and regular revolute petals; from both its large channelled coloured bracts distinguish it at first sight. Along with it will have to be placed the *Tillandsia heliconioides* of Kunth, a plant with the same peculiar habit and, as it appears from the description given of it by that author, the same peculiarities of structure; but differing in its leaves being narrower, awl-shaped at the point, the bracts flesh-coloured, and the flowers white, or nearly so."

It is an extremely pretty stove plant, for which we are indebted to C. B. Warner, Esq. It is said to be a native of the neighbourhood of Rio Janeiro. Fig. 1. represents a petal, with the two scales at its base; and it also shews how one of the stamens is inserted into the very base of the petal, between the scales, while the petals themselves are united by the stamens that are intermediate to them; fig. 2. shews a section of one of the scales, and indicates that they are adherent to the petals for more than half their length; fig. 3. is a section of the ovary.

In cultivation this requires to be potted in leaf mould, with a quantity of potsherds for drainage. Plenty of water should be given during the summer months, but sparingly in winter. Or it may be grown suspended in a wire basket, like an Orchidaceous plant. It is propagated by suckers.

The name commemorates the merits of Dr. de Vriese, Professor of Botany at Amsterdam, an excellent botanist and physiologist.

ISMENE *virescens*.

ISMENE VIRESCENS.

Greenish-flowered Ismene.

Nat. Ord. AMARYLLIDACEÆ.—AMARYLLIDS of Lindley.
Linnæan Class HEXANDRIA, Order MONOGYNIA.

ISMENE, Herbert.—Perianth corolline inferior, six-parted ; tube incurved cylindrical ; limb spreading, segments narrow-linear ; cup or coronet large exserted tubulose, twelve toothed the alternate teeth emarginate, bearing the stamens in the sinuses. *Stamens* six, filaments deflexedly conniving ; anthers attached scarcely below the middle. *Style* filiform ; *stigma* simple obtuse. *Ovary* inferior, three-celled ; *ovules* few erect. *Seeds* fleshy round green.

I. virescens ; leaves bright green erectish acute sheathing for a considerable length at the base ; scape two-edged ; ovary shortly stalked ; tube about as long as the segments ; lobes of the coronet shorter than the petals roundish toothed.

I. virescens, *Lindley in Bot. Reg.* 1841, t. 12.

A handsome greenhouse bulb, very nearly allied to Mr. Herbert's *I. pedunculata,* but the tube is longer, and there are no green stripes upon the coronet, neither do the leaves appear less sheathing at the base than in *I. Amancaes* as should occur in *Mr. Herbert's* plant. The flowers of the present although greenish white, have an agreeable lemon-like fragrance.

VOL. IV.—285   T

This plant first flowered in July 1841 in the garden of the Horticultural Society, having been received among other bulbs from Cusco, where it was found by Mr. Pentland.

The species grows well in a mixture of loam, peat, and sand, and flowers from June to August. The leaves wither soon after flowering, when it must be kept perfectly dry until spring. It will then begin to send forth young leaves, and remind the cultivator that it requires a plentiful supply of water to perfect its growth. It is easily multiplied by offsets which it produces in abundance.

" Absolute rest in winter is essential to this genus, which delights in very light sandy soil ; its cultivation is easy when those two requisites are observed. *I. Amancaes* seems to thrive best in pure white sand, at least in the vicinty of the bulb. I have flowered it in the open ground by putting a pot full of white sand with the bulbs into the border. *I. Calathina* is less particular as to soil, and *I. pedunculata* is hardier than either, vegetates in a lower temperature, and flags sooner in hot weather. They should be planted in a border of light compost in April, and the bulbs must be taken up when the leaf is cut by frost in November or sooner, without breaking off the thick fleshy fibres which will endure through the winter after the bulbs are taken off. They must be put in a box or large pot, and covered with dry sand or earth, and kept quite dry till the following April or May. If *I. Amancaes* be set in the stove at the beginning of May, and watered, it will flower immediately, and should be removed into a green-house as soon as the first bud is ready to expand. The seed of Ismene is large and round, and vegetates immediately in a remarkable manner, forming a bulb as big as itself (sometimes much bigger) far under ground without pushing any leaf. As soon as the seed rots, the young bulb must be left without water till the next spring. A person unaware of the peculiarity of this genus and *Choretis*, when he found the seed rotten, would be likely to throw away the earth without suspecting the formation of the bulb near the bottom of the pot. If the seedlings of *I. Amancaes* are grown in loam, I believe they will be twenty years before they attain size to flower; in pure white sand, or a very sandy compost, I think they may flower the third. (*Herb. Amar.* 223.)

The name Ismene is mythological.

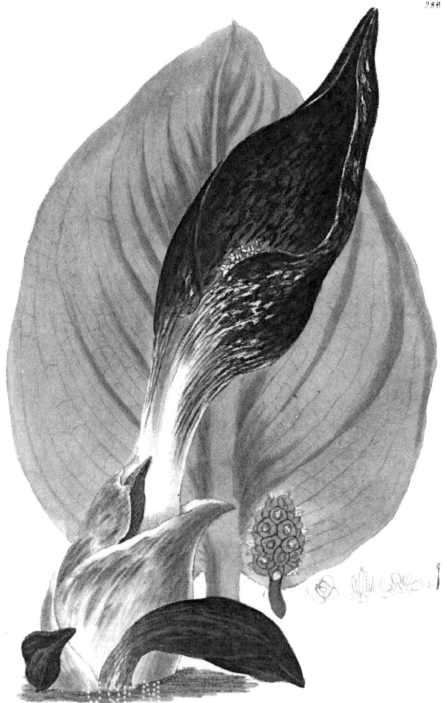

SYMPLOCARPUS foetidus

SYMPLOCARPUS FŒTIDUS.

Fœtid Symplocarpus, or Scunkweed.

Nat. Ord. Orontiaceæ.—Orontiads of Lindley.
Linnæan Class Hexandria, Order Monogynia.

SYMPLOCARPUS, Salisbury.—*Spathe* cucullate-conchiform acuminate ; *spadix* pedunculate subglobose, clothed with hermaphrodite flowers. *Perigone* tetraphyllous, at length baccate. *Stamens* four opposite the leaves of the perigone ; *filaments* linear, complanate, included ; *anthers* two-celled, the cells parallel. Ovary one-celled ; ovules one ; *style* tetragonal pyramidal ; *stigma* terminal minute. *Berries* coadunate, one-celled one-seeded. *Seeds* exalbuminous.

S. fœtidus.

S. fœtidus, *Salisbury in Trans. Hort. Soc. Sweet's Brit. Flow. Gard.* t. 57.

Dracontium fœtidum, *Willdenow Sp. pl.* 2, 281.

Pothos fœtida, *Bot. Mag.* t. 836.

A very curious stemless perennial. The leaves are large, smooth, pale green, often tinged with purple or brown, ovate-cordate, strongly veined, entire, preceded by conspicuous sheathing stipules, and protected by large glaucous spathulate-linguiform veinless bracts. The scapes are radical, appearing

286

before the leaves; the spathe discoloured ovoid roundish, cucullate, obliquely acuminate, its point coarctate plaited involutely auriculate at the base, thick and spongy, livid purple blotched and spotted with pale green or greenish yellow blotched with purple. The spadix pedunculate, simple, almost sphærical, covered with hermaphrodite flowers. The flowers are without bracts, tessellately imbricate, adnate. The perianth is four-parted, persistent, divided to the base, its segments cucullate, truncate, compressed at the apex, emarginate, at length becoming very thick and spongy. Stamens four, opposite the divisions of the perianth; filaments subulate, flat; anthers exserted, short, oblong-oval, two-celled. Style thick, pyramidal, quadrangular, acuminate; stigma simple, minute, pubescent, shorter than the stamens. Ovary immersed in the spongy receptacle, one-seeded. Seed naked, large, round, inclosed in the common receptacle. The conspicuous part of the plant is the spathe, not the true flowers which are enclosed by it, and are quite unattractive.

The seed of the *Symplocarpus* according to Nuttall, does not possess anything like a proper cotyledon, the embryo formed in the exact posture of the growing plant, (with the radical downwards,) differs not from it in any particular, but that of size. In place of a cotyledon there is a sheathing stipule similar to that which is ever after produced; in fact, it is viviparous.

This highly curious species is a native of North America, and is not very common in gardens. It blooms in March. The soil in which it should be grown is soft black peat, which is the kind of soil in which they naturally grow. They require a moist situation, as they are subaquatics. The inflorescence being so curious it is well worth cultivation in any collection, and its fine large light green leaves make a fine appearance after flowering. It is quite hardy, and may be increased by dividing at the root.

The name comes from *symploke*, connection, and *karpos*, fruit.

TRADESCANTIA *rosea.*

TRADESCANTIA ROSEA.

Rose-coloured Spiderwort.

Nat. Ord. COMMELYNACEÆ.—SPIDERWORTS of Lindley.
Linnæan Class HEXANDRIA, Order MONOGYNIA.

TRADESCANTIA, Linnæus.—Perianth deeply six-parted, three outer segments calycine persistent at length connivent, the three inner petaloid sessile persistent. *Stamens* six; filaments bearded or rarely glabrous the apex dilated into the connective; anther cells parallel margining the connective. *Ovary* three-celled; cells many-seeded; *style* filiform glabrous; stigma obtuse three cornered or suborbiculately dilated, obsoletely three-lobed. *Capsule* two-three-celled, loculicidally three-valved, the valves bearing the septa in the middle. *Seeds* few subquadrate peltate.

T. rosea; erect, leaves grass-like linear keeled acute glabrous, ciliated at the base; scape leafy; peduncles elongated erect; umbels many-flowered; perianth glabrous.

T. rosea, *Michaux Fl. Amer.* i. 193. *Sweet Brit. Flow. Gard.* t. 183.

A pretty hardy herbaceous perennial, with fleshy roots, throwing up numerous stalkless branches in a close tuft. The leaves are numerous crowded, linear grass-like, keeled on the lower side, and channelled on the upper, obsoletely lined, smooth, and dotted all over with innumerable minute dots; those of the stem fringed at the base where they clasp the

287

stem, with long white hairs. The scape is short leafy, smooth, slightly angular, producing several erect, cylindrical peduncles which are thickest at the base, and smooth. The umbels bear several flowers on smooth pedicels which lengthen out as the flower arrives at maturity, and are surrounded at the base by a fleshy transparent sheath, terminated in unequal teeth. The perianth is deeply six-parted; the three outer leaflets calyx-like, oval, concave, scarcely acute, of a brownish green colour; the three inner ones petal-like, spreading, broadly ovate, acute, more or less undulate and crenulate, over-lapping at the base, of a pale rose colour. Stamens six, spreading; filaments fringed at the base with long jointed purple hairs, the upper part smooth; anthers two-lobed, crescent-shaped; pollen bright yellow. Ovary smooth and glossy; style smooth, white, shorter than the filaments; stigma capitate, papillose.

This pretty perennial plant is a native of North America, and is scarce in collections, though certainly deserving a place in them. Our figure was taken from a plant which bloomed in the nursery of Mr. Dennis, at Chelsea, in September, and it continued to produce its flowers in abundance till the end of October.

It thrives best in a soil composed chiefly of peat; but having a little light turfy loam mixed with it, and being a dwarf growing plant, is most proper for the front of the flower borders, where it will soon form a good tuft, and will be seen to most advantage. It may be increased by dividing at the root.

TRADESCANTIA iridescens

TRADESCANTIA IRIDESCENS.

Iridescent Tradescantia.

——◆——

Nat. Ord. COMMELYNACEÆ.—SPIDERWORTS of Lindley.
Linnæan Class HEXANDRIA, Order MONOGYNIA.

———————

TRADESCANTIA, Linnæus.—*Perianth* deeply six-parted, three outer segments calycine persistent at length connivent, the three inner petaloid
sessile persistent. *Stamens* six; filaments bearded or rarely glabrous
the apex dilated into the connective; anther cells parallel margining
the connective. *Ovary* three-celled; cells many-seeded; *style* filiform
glabrous; stigma obtuse three cornered or suborbiculately dilated,
obsoletely three-lobed. *Capsule* two-three-celled, loculicidally three-
valved, the valves bearing the septa in the middle. *Seeds* few subquadrate peltate.

———————

T. iridescens ; stemless with fleshy roots; leaves oblong acute concave, glabrous ciliated hairy beneath, umbels lax terminal sessile; petals obovate three times longer than the stems.

T. iridescens, *Lindley in Bot. Reg.* 1838, *misc.* 160; and 1840, t. 34.

———————

This is a very pretty stemless herbaceous plant. The
leaves which spread nearly flat, are ovate-lanceolate acute,
thick and fleshy with a semitransparent appearance; they are
smooth and of a shining green above, paler with short
brownish hairs beneath, and fringed or ciliated on the margin.
The flowers are numerous, surrounded by the leaves, and
opening in succession in bunches of six or eight at a time; in
cloudy weather they remain expanded all day, but in bright
sunny weather they close and decay before noon. The sepals
are pale green ovate-oblong, the petals larger and spreading
roundish ovate tapering a little to the base, and of a bright
reddish purple. The filaments are about half the length of

288

the petals and of a deeper purple, hairy at the base. The style is not quite so long as the filaments.

The accompanying drawing was made from a plant that flowered in the garden of Sir Charles Lemon, Bart. at Carclew in Cornwall. It is a native of Mexico, near the Real del Monte mines, whence it was sent to Carclew in 1838.

It is a half-hardy perennial with tuberous roots growing in any rich soil, and flowering in July and August, each flower only lasting for a few hours. The plant is increased freely by seeds, but seldom flowers before the second season; its roots may be preserved during the winter, if kept dry in the pots, or in sand, like Cape bulbs.

Although its flowers are very ephemeral there is a long succession of them, and their iridescent appearance renders them extremely pretty.

Tradescantia is named in honour of John Tradescant gardener to King Charles I.

CPSIA information can be obtained at www.ICGtesting.com
Printed in the USA
BVOW07s1728040314

346645BV00009B/227/P